1·25

Pelican Book A1029
The Dialectics of Liberation

The Dialectics of Liberation

Edited by David Cooper

Penguin Books

Penguin Books Ltd, Harmondsworth,
Middlesex, England
Penguin Books Inc., 7110 Ambassador Road,
Baltimore, Maryland 21207, U.S.A.
Penguin Books Australia Ltd, Ringwood,
Victoria, Australia

First published 1968
Copyright © Penguin Books Ltd, 1968

Made and printed in Great Britain by
C. Nicholls & Company Ltd
Set in Linotype Granjon

Contents

Introduction

The Congress on the Dialectics of Liberation was held in London at the Roundhouse in Chalk Farm from 15 July to 30 July 1967. The present volume is a compilation of some of the principal addresses delivered on this occasion. I would like to outline in this brief introduction how the Congress came about and in particular why we, the organizers, arranged this meeting between these particular people, why we generated this curious pastiche of eminent scholars and political activists.

The organizing group consisted of four psychiatrists who were very much concerned with radical innovation in their own field – to the extent of their counter-labelling their discipline as anti-psychiatry. The four were Dr R. D. Laing and myself, also Dr Joseph Berke and Dr Leon Redler. Our experience originated in studies into that predominant form of socially stigmatized madness that is called schizophrenia. Most people who are called mad and who are socially victimized by virtue of that attribution (by being 'put away', being subjected to electric shocks, tranquillizing drugs, and brain-slicing operations, and so on) come from family situations in which there is a desperate need to find some scapegoat, someone who will consent at a certain point of intensity in the whole transaction of the family group to take on the disturbance of each of the others and, in some sense, suffer for them. In this way the scapegoated person would become a diseased object in the family system and the family system would involve medical accomplices in its machinations. The doctors would be used to attach the label 'schizophrenia' to the diseased object and then systematically set about the destruction of that object by the physical and social processes that are termed 'psychiatric treatment'.

All this seemed to us to relate to certain political facts in the world around us. One of the principal facts of this sort was the war of the United States against the Vietnamese people. In this latter situation there seemed to us to be a violent transformation of the idea of 'the enemy'. Firstly, the enemy became transformed into the 'inhuman': that is to say, men who embodied all the most detested and therefore externalized attributes of the 'men' – qualities such as underhandedness, cunning, meanness (the conservation of their supplies and supply-lines), 'violence' (the wish to shit on 'us'), and 'rape' (the tearing apart of the Western-imposed family pattern – with its neat analogue, the oriental brothel).

I recently met in Cuba a Vietnamese guerilla commandant who talked about how, while he was conducting an operation against the invading U.S. and mercenary forces, he knew that his wife and three children were being slaughtered in the next village. He knew that and yet he dispassionately and successfully carried out his military or counter-military work. This man acted by choice in a way that conscripted U.S. soldiers never can do – they simply lose and are lost to their families and can never give anything up. One human fact that generates most terror in the first world, the Imperialist World, is the fact of choice, the beginning of freedom, of spontaneous self-assertion of persons or a whole people. For this reason, among others, the 'free' opponent must be categorized as 'inhuman'.

After the conversion, on these lines, of man into the 'inhuman', there is a further subtle metamorphosis. The 'inhuman' become 'non-human'. At this point they become the ultimate projected versions of ourselves, those bits of ourselves that we wish most finally to destroy in order to become Pure Being. If we cannot destroy these bits in ourselves, we have to destroy them in this outside version. The 'sub-human' or 'non-human' are totally destructible (witness a similar process with 'Abo'-hunting, continued well into this century in Australia), and there can be no possibility of guilt. They have to be wiped out almost before they exist as the non-human in our metaphysical imaginations. They are of course wiped out by their being what they are – which, of course, is what they are not. They just need some sort of *coup de grâce* wrapped up in napalm. Then, we believe, we shall know where we are. Or we shall know where *they* are – in *our* graves!

At the Congress, to bridge the gap between theory and practice, we invited people such as Gregory Bateson, Herbert Marcuse and Lucien Goldmann to represent the theoretical pole (in the best Greek sense of this term where theory is *theoria* or contemplation), and Stokely Carmichael, who is an activist in the most real sense of that term.

This book is centrally concerned with the analysis destruction – destruction in two senses: firstly, the self-destruction of the human species by racism (Carmichael), by greed (Gerassi on Imperialism), by the erosion of our ecological context (Bateson, Goodman), by blind, frightened repression of natural instinctuality (Marcuse), by illusion and mystification (Laing and myself); secondly, closely interwoven with the first sense, these essays study the human conditions under which men destroy each other (Jules Henry's essay on Psychological Preparation for War in particular explored this subject). So it is a book about mass suicide and mass murder and we have to achieve at least a minimal clarity about the 'mechanisms' by which these processes operate before we begin to talk about liberation. However, in each of the essays I have included there are at least strong hints as to how this liberation might be achieved.

It seems to me that a cardinal failure of all past revolutions has been the dissociation of liberation on the mass social level, i.e. liberation of whole classes in economic and political terms, and liberation on the level of the individual and the concrete groups in which he is directly engaged. If we are to talk of revolution today our talk will be meaningless unless we effect some union between the macro-social and micro-social, and between 'inner reality' and 'outer reality'. We have only to think back about the personal factor in Lenin that made it possible for him to ignore so much of the manoeuvrings of the super-bureaucrat Stalin until it was too late. We have only to consider the limited *personal* liberation achieved in the 'Second World' (The Soviet Union and Eastern Europe). Then we get the point that a radical de-bourgeoisification of society has to be achieved in the very style of revolutionary work and is not automatically entailed by the seizure of power by an exploited class. We must never forget that conditions of scarcity inhibit – though not neces-sarily prohibit – personal liberation in this sense. But in the First World we have conditions of potential affluence which must be grasped and realized.

If we are to search for possible paradigmatic instances of this conjunction in the world, the most immediate situations seem to be those in Cuba, already liberated, and Vietnam, inexorably on the way to liberation. Both countries are forced to *continue* their revolutions in the face of outside aggres-sion. China on this issue is less certain, but one of the mean-ings of the cultural revolution seems to be the diffusion of power from artificial hierarchies (where the people concerned are figments) into the minds and hands of actual people. Isolated, they too seem to be *continuing* their revolution.

So I think what our Congress was all about was not the dishing up of solutions to world problems already prepared, but an opportunity to think the thing out together. This is why the 'principal speakers' mixed so freely and spontan-eously with the 'audience'. It is why so many young people actually took to living in the Round-house and then took their seminars out into local pubs, cafés and public places. This was really the founding event of the Antiuniversity of London which now functions full-time, carrying over the spirit of the Congress in what may be a permanent form.

At the Congress we were concerned with new ways in which intellectuals might act to change the world, ways in which we might move beyond the 'intellectual masturbation' of which Stokely Carmichael accuses us. We recognized that radical groups in the First World had been conventionally split – not only ideological but on personal lines. There is always some sort of spurious messiah who arouses hope and then disappoints hope. This is not the 'fault' of the 'messiah' – it is the fault of 'hope'. Hope has to have another appointment. Not now and not then, but some other time, its own time – which is our time.

We have to take over time and own it.

D.C.

Institute of Phenomenological Studies

4 St George's Terrace

London NW3

The Obvious | R. D. Laing

... a recent study of the American public's view of U.S. policy towards China (prepared for the Council on Foreign Relations by the Survey Research Center at the University of Michigan) reports that one out of every four Americans still does not know that the Chinese people have a communist government.[1]

I would not be surprised if over half of those of us who know that the people of China have a communist government, do *not* know that one quarter of the population do *not*, if this report is to be believed.

I want to draw attention to a few of those features of North American and European society that seem to be most dangerous, because they seem to help, or perhaps even to be necessary, to maintain and to perpetuate our component of a social world system that as a whole presents more and more the appearance of total irrationality.

To a considerable extent what follows is an essay in stating what I take to be obvious. It is obvious that the social world situation is endangering the future of all life on this planet. To state the obvious is to share with you what (in your view) my misconceptions might be. The obvious can be dangerous. The deluded man frequently finds his delusions so obvious that he can hardly credit the good faith of those who do not share them. Hitler regarded it as perfectly obvious that the Jews were a poison to the Aryan race and hence required to be exterminated. What is obvious to Lyndon Johnson is not at all obvious to Ho Chi Minh. What is obvious to me might not be obvious to anyone else. The obvious is literally that which stands in one's way, in front of or over against oneself. One has to begin by recognizing that it exists for oneself.

This talk is also an attempt to exhibit for your inspection some facets of my present effort to dia-gnose, to see into and through social reality. I at most am presuming to try to articulate what seems to me to be the case, in some very limited aspects, in respect of what is going on in the human sector of the planet. I shall have to deal for the most part in generalities. I am not sure whether these are clichés to many of you. One man's revolution is another's platitude.

The invisibility of social events

The study of social events presents an almost insurmountable difficulty, in that their visibility, as one might say, is very low. In social *space* one's direct immediate capacity to see what is happening does not extend any further than one's own senses extend. Beyond that one has to make inferences based on hearsay evidence, reports of one kind or another of what other human beings are able to see within *their* equally limited field of observation. As in space, so in *time*. Our capacity to probe back into history is extraordinarily limited. Even in the most detailed investigations of small fragments of micro-history, in studies of families, one finds it difficult to get past two or three generations. Beyond that, how things have come to be as they are disappears into mist.

They often go out of view in space and time at a boundary between here and now, and there and then – a boundary which unfortunately consigns here and now to unintelligibility without information from there and then, which is, however, beyond our reach.

Context of social events

A fundamental lesson that almost all social scientists have learned is that the intelligibility of social events requires that they be always seen in a context that extends both spatially and in time. The dilemma is that this is often as impossible as it is necessary. The fabric of sociality is an interlaced set of contexts, of sub-systems interlaced with other sub-systems, of contexts interlaced with metacontexts and metametacontexts and so on until it reaches a theoretical limit, the context of all possible social contexts, comprising together with all the contexts that are subsumed within it, what one might call the *total social world system*. Beyond this total social world system – as there is no larger social context that we can define – there is no further *social* context to which one can refer the intelligibility of the total social world system.

As we begin from micro-situations and work up to macro-situations we find that the apparent irrationality of behaviour on a small scale takes on a certain form of intelligibility when one sees it in context. One moves, for example, from the apparent irrationality of the single 'psychotic' individual to the intelligibility of that irrationality within the context of the family. The irrationality of the family in its turn must be placed within the context of its encompassing networks. These further networks must be seen within the context of yet larger organizations and institutions. These larger contexts do not exist out there on some periphery of social space: they pervade the interstices of all that is comprised by them.

The paradox of the irrationality of the whole

It is terrifying that having moved up through the irration-ality/rationality of sets of sub-systems until we reach the total social context, we there seem to glimpse a total system that appears to be dangerously out of the control of the sub-systems or sub-contexts that comprise it. Here we face a theoretical, logical and practical dilemma. Namely, we seem to arrive at an empirical limit which itself appears to be without obvious intelligibility, and beyond this limiting context we do not know what further context there may be that may help us to set the total social world system in a larger pattern or design in which it finds its rationality. Some people think that it may be possible to do this within a cosmic pattern. On the other hand, more than one person has said – and usually been regarded as mad for having said it – that perhaps God is not dead: perhaps God is Himself mad.

Mediations

We have a theoretical and practical problem of finding the mediations between the different levels of contexts: between the different systems and metasystems, extending all the way from the smallest micro- to the largest macro-social systems. The intermediate systems that lie on this range have to be studied not only in themselves, but as conditioning and conditioned media between the individual parts and the whole.*

In our society, at certain times, this interlaced set of systems may lend itself to revolutionary change, not at the extreme micro or macro ends; that is, not through the individual pirouette of solitary repentance on the one hand, or by a seizure of the machinery of the state on the other; but by sudden, structural, radical qualitative changes in the intermediate system levels: changes in a factory, a hospital, a school, a university, a set of schools, or a whole area of industry, medicine, education, etc.

* For examples of such a study, see Jules Henry's essay later in this volume.

The example of psychiatry

I started to try to see through the dense opacity of social events from the study of certain people who were labelled psychotic or neurotic, as seen in mental hospitals, psychiatric units and out-patient clinics. I began to see that I was involved in the study of *situations* and not simply of individuals. It seemed (and this still seems to be the case) that the study of such situations was arrested in three principal ways. In the first place the behaviour of such people was regarded as signs of a pathological process that was going on *in* them, and only secondarily of anything else. The whole subject was enclosed in a medical metaphor. In the second place this medical metaphor conditioned the conduct of all those who were enclosed by it, doctors and patients. Thirdly, through this metaphor the person who was the patient in the system, being isolated from the system, could no longer be seen as a person: as a corollary, it was also difficult for the doctor to behave as a person. A person does not exist without a social context. You cannot take a person out of his social context and still see him as a person, or *act* towards him as a person. If one does not *act* towards the other as a person, one de-personalizes *oneself*.

Someone is gibbering away on his knees, talking to some-one who is not there. Yes, he is praying. If one does not ac-cord him the social intelligibility of this behaviour, he can only be seen as mad. Out of social context, his behaviour can only be the outcome of an unintelligible 'psychological' and/or 'physical' process, for which he requires treatment. This metaphor sanctions a massive ignorance of the social context within which the person was interacting. It also renders any genuine reciprocity between the process of label-ling (the practice of psychiatry) and of being labelled (the role of patient) as impossible to conceive as it is to observe. Someone whose mind is imprisoned in the metaphor cannot see it as a metaphor. It is just *obvious*. How, he will say, can diagnosing someone as ill who is obviously ill, make him ill? Or make him better, for that matter? Some of us began to realize that this aspect of the theory and practice of psychiatry was an essay in non-dialectical thinking and practice. However, once one had got oneself out of the straightjacket of this metaphor, it was possible to see the function of this anti-dialectical exercise. The unintelligibility of the experience and behaviour of the diagnosed person is created by the person diagnosing him, as well as by the person diagnosed. This stratagem seems to serve specific functions within the structure of the system in which it occurs.

To work smoothly, it is necessary that those who use this stratagem do not themselves know that it is a stratagem. They should not be cynical or ruthless: they should be sincere and concerned. Indeed, the more 'treatment' is escalated – through negotiation (psychotherapy), pacification (tranquillization), physical struggle (cold-packs and straitjackets), through at one and the same time more and more *humane* and *effective* forms of destruction (electroshocks and insulin comas), to the final solution of cutting a person's brain in two or more slices by psycho-surgery – the more the human beings who do these things to other people tend to feel sincere concern, dedication, pity; and they can hardly help but feel more and more indignant, sorrowful, horrified and scandalized at those of their colleagues who are horrified and scandalized by their actions. As for the patients, the more they protest, the less insight they display; the more they fight back, clearly the more they need to be pacified; the more persecuted they feel at being destroyed, the more necessary to destroy them. And at the end of it all, they may indeed be 'cured', they may even express gratitude for no longer having the brains left to protest against persecution. But many do not. This only goes to show, as one leading psychiatrist said to me: 'It's the white man's burden, Ronald. We can't expect any thanks, but we must go on.'

Hundreds of thousands of people are involved in this amazing political operation. Many patients in their innocence continue to flock for help to psychiatrists who honestly feel they are giving people what they ask for: relief from suffering. This is but one example of the diametric irrationality of much of our social scene. The *exact* opposite is achieved to what is intended. Doctors in all ages have made fortunes by killing their patients by means of their cures. The difference in psychiatry is that it is the death of the soul.

Those who think they have seen through this to some extent see it as a system of violence and counter-violence. People called brain surgeons have stuck knives into the brains of hundreds and thousands of people in the last twenty years: people who may never have used a knife against anyone themselves; they may have broken a few windows, sometimes screamed, but they have killed fewer people than the rest of the population, many many fewer if we count the mass-exterminations of wars, declared and undeclared, waged by the legalized 'sane' members of our society.

Such institutionalized, organized violence seems to begin to be called into play at certain moments in a micro-political power struggle, often but not necessarily involving a family, always involving a network of people, more or less extended. The apparent irrationality and sometimes apparently senseless violence of one person in this group – not necessarily the 'patient' – finds its intelligibility in the social context. This apparently senseless violence is a moment in an ongoing set of reciprocals of violence and counterviolence. However, the worst violence of all is the reciprocal denial of reciprocity, the creation of a frozen, non-dialectical *im-*

passe, both by the patient who refuses to communicate, and by the psychiatrist, who double-stamps this *refusal* as *inability*.

To cut a long story very short: the context of the individual at first appears as his immediate network, and the contexts of that network come into view as larger social frameworks that have not by any means been adequately identified. However, we can theoretically reach farther than our empirical research can go, in the hope that our theoretical reach can help us to extend our practical grasp. So we may postulate that there is no end to context upon context until one reaches a total social world system which comprises a hierarchy of contexts, metacontexts, metametacontexts: interlaced patterns of control, frequently violent control, no part of which is understandable if extrapolated from the whole of which it is a part. Nevertheless, some components of this do seem to be more irremediably irrational* than others.

I sometimes think that the danger of the interlaced sets of psychiatric systems in our society (to their homeostasis, equilibrium, steady state) is not where most people in the system suppose it to be. In the mental-health field there is some anxiety lest we may not have enough mental hospitals, research workers, nurses, etc. to cope with the continued increase in the incidence of mental illness, so-called. It may be that the problem is not that there will be too *few* psychiatrists for too many patients, but that there will be *too*

---

*An action can be regarded as irrational if it is ostensibly a means towards an end, such that this means leads to an end it purports to avoid. One attempts to avoid an outcome by certain means. Such means are irrational when they bring about the end they are intended to avoid – a common finding in the psychoanalysis of 'neurotic' defence against anxiety. The defences generate the anxieties they are defences against. I am putting in parenthesis the question of the rationality of the end.

few patients coming along in the next ten or twenty years.

It may be that what our system needs is a sufficient number of people to be elected patients and treated accordingly. To each network of perhaps 20 or 30 people some sort of human lightning conductor may be required into which 'bad vibrations' from unlived living may be channelled – a sort of human earthing device. In the intermediate zone we appear to deal with our violence by such elective focusing (scapegoating being but one obvious example). This is not only in terms of psychiatry. Think how networks selectively funnel people into the criminal channel. On the intermediate levels between macro and micro we see all the time how one out of so many people is nominated as he or she who is felt to epitomize a violence that justifies violence from US. It is plausible to me that this represents a desperate stratagem to keep the system ongoing. If this sounds a bit mad to you, you will be not entirely wrong. This is the type of theory that psychiatric patients often bring forward. They are labelled psychotic partly *because* they bring forward this type of theory.

I have so far sketched some ways violence may be *focused* on single persons. Let us now look at the other end of the scale, the macro end of the intermediate zone. Here violence is projected in an antithetical way, not on any individual *within* the system, but on some vague mass being *outside* the subsystem – THEM. Here we are concerned with the massive actions of the largest groups of people in the world. I want to consider for a moment some facets of the macro-situation. Again, I am going to state only what seems to me obvious, for the same reasons I gave before: that it might not be obvious to others and it will give you the opportunity to make up your minds as to how misguided or naïve I am.

Looking at the whole world scene, it seems that transecting

existing human divisions and struggles in terms of race, nationality or geopolitical blocs a new transworld polarization is rapidly occurring between Haves and Have-nots. Most of the Have-nots are peasants. Their age-long misery seems to be more in the process of being deepened by the minority of the Haves than otherwise. It seems that an increasing number of the Have-nots are beginning to become restive and to be no longer resigned to this state of affairs. Armed struggles are current in Asia, Latin America and Africa. As far as I know the Have-nots do not tend to look to the U.S.A. or Western Europe for help, although their governments (who belong to the Haves) may do so. The Have-notes are not sophisticated in Western economics. Rightly or wrongly, I have formed the impression that many of them have begun to feel that the U.S.A. and Western Europe have been exploiting them for too long. They look, rightly or wrongly, to Russia, to an increasing extent to China, and to a growing extent to themselves for their help. Looking at this situation, on a worldwide scale, it seems to me as though a World War (World Wars I and II being the prodromata of the real global involvement) is well under way. The world revolution, Arnold Toynbee has suggested, has begun. But who will eventually be fighting whom is still not clear. Ten years from now the U.S.A. and China may be in alliance against Africa. Provisionally, for the time being, it seems that *our* slice of the world cake (since practically all of us here are from Western Europe or the U.S.A.) has a certain homogeneity despite the heterogeneity of very intricate interlacing of its multiple subsystems, and despite its plurality of contradictions. But many of these contradictions are more apparent than real. They arise from our belief in our own lies and mystifications. Many people are tortured by contradictions that exist only between facts and propaganda, not in the facts themselves. For instance, we have *not* abolished poverty within our own territory; the U.S.A. is *not* a democracy. Once you do not think that the U.S.A. is a democracy, then there are a great many problems that do not have to be solved because they do not exist. Many people in the U.K. still believe that the U.K. is one of the most peace-loving countries in the world. It has fought more wars, I believe, in the last 300 years than any other nation on earth.

I am not going to enumerate the mystifications to which I think we are subject. I shall take most of that for granted. I find no problem in the fact that a growing number of the people in Africa, Asia, Latin America – the local inhabitants (called, by *us*, terrorists) – are fighting against the white invaders of their countries. This violence is not problematical. Where is the problem? What does puzzle me somewhat, however, is that the spokesmen of the U.S.A. and of this country sometimes seem to think that the violence of the inhabitants of Latin America, Asia and Africa can only be explained as the outcome of a communist plot to overthrow the U.S.A. and Europe.

Suppose the Chinese had 600,000 troops in Southern Mexico engaged in slaughtering the local inhabitants, devastating the ecology and dropping more bombs on Northern Mexico each month than were dropped on the whole of Germany during the whole of World War II. Suppose the Chinese had encircled the U.S.A. with missile bases in Canada, Cuba, the Pacific Islands; that China's fleets patrolled the seas and its atomic submarines appeared to be ubiquitous; and that all this was deployed, according to the Chinese, for no other purpose than directly to put down a threat to the Chinese people by the people of the U.S.A. And suppose that China had made it quite clear into the bargain that it regarded the U.S.A. as the greatest threat to world peace, and that if the U.S.A. sent any troops into Northern Mexico, they would give them all they'd got and smash them back into the Stone Age.[2] Then I would have no difficulty in understanding the anxieties of the people of the U.S.A. and its leaders about such a policy of 'containment', whether or not they were aware that the people of China had a communist government.

But that is not what we have got to understand. We can more profitably exercise ourselves by trying to understand how the statements of the leaders of the U.S.A. often seem to attribute to the Chinese precisely the policy they themselves seem to be pursuing towards the Chinese.

In Vietnam several million men, women and children, mainly peasants, are exposed to indiscriminate death and mutilation. When they fight, they are fighting on their own land for their own land. On the other side, thousands of miles away from their homes, are mercenaries, well-paid, well-fed, steel-trained specialists in the technology of killing. There are people fighting to destroy all forms of life over a sector of the earth's surface, because somewhere in that space there may be some human beings who have inside them the 'wrong' ideology.[3]

We do not have to ask why an increasing number of the world's inhabitants hate us Europeans and the U.S.A. We do not have to go into extraordinary psychological explanations of why I would hate someone who had napalmed my children. It is no more complicated than black and white.

Consider Vietnam again. It is not at all obvious why it is going on. No purely economic explanation seems adequate. It may be imperialism gone mad (Cooper*). U Thant has proposed that it is a sort of Holy War. The theoreticians in the Pentagon say that it is a global operation in order to contain the advance of communist imperialism. It may be much more primitive. President Johnson says to combat commanders in the Officers' Mess at Qumran Bay: 'Come home with that coonskin on the wall.'[2] One hears extraordinary statements from U.S. politicians, such as 'Bringing

* See page 200.

Red China to her knees'. What we have here is the most primitive analogical 'thinking', behind which lies a hinterland of fantasy one hardly dares contemplate.

Many people feel ashamed and disgusted by Vietnam. Nevertheless, some of us have to grasp the full implications of the fact that a great number of people have got to the state where they feel guilty if they are turned down by the draft; that a great number of people feel ashamed and guilty if they *don't* manufacture, deliver or drop napalm, etc.

This whole system and the eager and active human perpetuation of it is almost beyond comprehension, because it defies imagination if one is not in it, and its horror is so stark that it is almost unbearable if one is in it.

Multiple ignorance

Moreover, the system itself generates ignorance of itself, and ignorance of this ignorance. I would guess that *at least* three out of four of the three quarters of Americans whom we are assured are aware that the Chinese people have a communist government would not believe this figure. Let us suppose that one in four do not know – and do not know they do not know. Let us suppose that three out of four of the remainder do not know that one out of four does not know he does not know. So how many sane men can we address?

But this is just the beginning. Three out of four *do* know that the people of China have a communist government – and By God we better do something about it before it is too late: we must contain it, if not destroy it, before It destroys Us. I would guess that *at least* three quarters of the three quarters who 'know' that the people of China have a communist government have a reflex of horror and terror at the thought. But perhaps the worst of all reflexes is *pity*: 'How can we sit idly by and let this happen to our brothers and sisters the Chinese. Look what they did to our missionaries – you can't blame them *all* for that of course. Dear Chiang, he did his best.'

The dear little old lady investor in tennis shoes has her nephew the General. He thinks she is too soft. She has always thought more of others than herself. 'I believe that a people gets the government it deserves. Look at our country for example. If the Chinese have a communist government it must be their fault to some extent – you can't just let them get away with that. If they don't want to get what's coming to them, they know what to do about it.'

There are those who know they don't know, those who don't know they don't know, and legions of those who find denser and denser realms of darkness in which to veil their own ignorance from themselves. And there are those who, no matter what they think they know or don't know to any metalevel, will *just do what they are told* when it comes to the bit. Those that are left, who know they don't know and who will not necessarily do what they are told – it is to them that this speech is addressed, which I hope may be of some service, if only as a joke, to the last surviving *human beings* on the planet. The privilege of being one of this number I hardly dare claim.

Once you are hooked you don't know you are hooked. One comes to be ashamed of one's original nature, terrified of it, and ready to destroy evidence of it in oneself and any-one else. This has been achieved – one can see it being achieved – not only by families but by all the institutions that are brought to bear on children. First, in babies, through the kinesics of handling and the suppression of their im-mediate instinctive intelligence of smell and touch and taste; thereafter through kinesics and *para*-linguistics – words are of tertiary significance. The product of this is a young man of eighteen who is ripe to volunteer to be (or at the very least to acquiesce in being) a hired killer. Who is *proud* to be processed to be a hired killer, deeply guilty and ashamed of himself if he is frightened, *even* in his guts, and guilty and ashamed if he feels guilty and ashamed of killing simply because he is told to do so.

For far too long psychologists have given a disproportionate amount of time and effort to the psychopathology of the abnormal. We need to catch up on the *normal* psychological correlates of the *normal* state of affairs, of which Vietnam is only one of the most obvious *normal* manifestations. I shall give you an example, a story of a type which has been told me so often that I regard it as only slightly excessively normal. A boy of three is held by his mother out of a sixth-storey window by his neck. His mother says: 'See how much I love you.' The demonstration being that if she did not love him she would drop him.

One could go through many speculations as to why a woman could be so warped as to terrorize her own son in such a way. When one has been through all that, one comes back, I think, to the obvious: the reason why she was doing this to him was exactly the reason she gave him. It was to show him that she loved him. Why else should she do it? That is what she said she was doing it for, and evidently to her no clearer proof of love could be vouchsafed. In that case, one has got to move into the psychology of that woman, and that is the psychology of normality. This is an example of *extreme normality*. The *normal* way parents get their children to love them is to terrorize them, to say to them in effect: 'Because I am not dropping you, because I am not killing you, this shows that I love you, and therefore you should come for the assuagement of your terror to the person who is generating the terror that you are seeking to have assuaged.' The above mother is rather hyper-normal.

To understand her one has to go back to her parents. Let us suppose she really meant what she said. She was doing this to the child in order to show him that she loved him. She has remained constantly puzzled and hurt that he did not exhibit the gratitude she would expect for taking this trouble. Other children are grateful when their parents do a lot *less* for them than *we* have done for you. What did her mother do to her? In what way did her mother not love her? Possibly her mother never held her out of a high window and showed her how much she loved her, as she should have done. And why not? You have to ask what her great-grandmother did or did not do for her grandmother, and so on.

The whole system, in any of its aspects, is so well into such multi-generational spiral effects that it is very difficult to see how the spiral can be turned round. The psychoanalyst Winnicott recently posed the question: One looks into the mirror to see oneself — what antecedes the mirror?[4] He suggests that what comes before the mirror is one's mother's face. So that if one's mother's face is a mirror, when one looks in one's mother's face one sees oneself. What else can one see? That is fine so long as one's mother, in looking at oneself, sees oneself. But if in looking at oneself she sees herself — sees oneself as an extension of herself, but in so doing is unaware of so doing, so that she *thinks* she sees oneself — out of that deep spiral of misapprehension however is one to find oneself again? Nor is it *herself* that she sees in the baby. She is seeing what her mother saw, and her mother saw, and so on. The spiral of alienation goes whirling back, way out of sight. And by the time one has lost oneself in the nth turn of this spiral of alienation and grown up to see, without knowing that one sees, one's mirror image in the face of one's enemy; to become the Other to an Other who is himself Other than himself; then we are just beginning to get to the precondition of the possibility of the amazing collective paranoid projective systems that operate on large scales. We attribute to Them exactly what We are doing to Them. Because We are seeing ourselves in Them, but we do not know that we are. We think that They are Them, but They are actually Us.

For instance, one of the ironies of history: 'All men are created equal. They are endowed by their creator with certain inalienable rights: among these are life, liberty and the pursuit of happiness.' It is the opening sentence of the Declaration of Independence of the Democratic Republic of Vietnam.

Can we find some way of disarticulating the circuit somewhere from within? We might be able to consider what are the weakest, what the strongest threads that maintain the tapestry in its tightly woven state.

I was struck by a remark that Sir Julian Huxley made to me a few years ago. He said he thought the most dangerous link in the chain was *obedience*. That we have been trained, and we train our children, so that we and they are prepared to do practically anything if told to do it by a sufficient authority. It is always said, 'it couldn't happen here', but it is always happening here.* It is particularly important to study the nature of obedience. Our system operates through a network of common-obedience reciprocities. What is the organization structure of this net? Clearly we have not all equal discretion in the exercise of power. In an ultimate sense we may wish to take on equal responsibility, but there is a vast differential in power in all sectors of the total world system. The people who exercise power can do so only if people carry out their orders. We have the spectacle at this very moment in the earth's history of white troops in the middle of jungle darkness blazing away at the darkness, for reasons they do not know – except that if they were forced to, I would think they would probably come down to saying, 'Well, ours is not to reason why. We are carrying

* *No doubt,* it is happening *there* as well.

out orders.' Some of them want to be heroes. I do not think many of them do.

The following is a simple morality tale from Yale University, an experiment conducted by Dr Stanley Milgram.[5]

Dr Milgram recruited 40 male volunteers who believed they were to take part in an experimental study of memory and learning at Yale University. The 40 men were between the ages of 20 and 50 and represented a wide range of occupations. Typical subjects were postal clerks, high school teachers, salesmen, engineers and laborers. One subject had not finished elementary school, but some others had doctorate and other professional degrees.

The role of experimenter was played by a 31-year-old high school teacher of biology. His manner was impassive but he maintained a somewhat stern appearance during the experiment. The experimenter was aided by a mild-mannered and likable man, who acted as a 'victim'. The experimenter interviewed each volunteer and, with him, the 'victim' masquerading as another volunteer. He told the two of them that the intention was to investigate the effects of punishment on learning, and in particular the differential effects of varying degrees of punishment and various types of teacher. The drawing of lots was rigged so that the volunteer was always the teacher and the 'victim' was always the learner. The victim was strapped into an 'electric chair' apparatus and electrode paste and an electrode were applied. The teacher-volunteer was then taken into an adjacent room and placed before a complex instrument labeled 'Shock Generator'. The teacher-volunteer was given a 45-volt shock to demonstrate the apparent authenticity of the machine.

Pulling the Switch

A row of 30 switches on the 'shock generator' were labeled from 15 to 450 volts by 15-volt steps. In addition, groups of switches were labeled from 'slight shock' to 'danger: severe shock'. Following instructions and in the context of a mock learning experiment, the teacher-volunteer was led to believe that he was administering increasingly more severe punishment to the learner-victim, who made prearranged responses. The learner-victim gave incorrect answers to three out of every four questions and received shocks as punishment for his errors. When the punitive shock reached the 300-volt level, the learner-victim – as had been prearranged – kicked on the wall of the room in which he was bound to the electric chair. At this point teacher-volunteers turned to the experimenter for guidance. The teacher-volunteer was advised to continue after a 5-10 second pause. After the 315-volt shock, the pounding was heard again. Silence followed. At this point in the experiment the teacher-volunteers began to react in various ways. But they were verbally encouraged, and even ordered in a firm manner, to proceed right up to the maximum level of voltage.

Test Results

... Dr Milgram states that contrary to all expectations 26 of the 40 subjects completed the series, finally administering 450 volts to the now silent 'victim'. Only 5 refused to carry on after the victim's first protest when 300-volts were apparently administered. Many continued, even though they experienced considerable emotional disturbance, as clearly shown by their spoken comments, profuse sweating, tremor, stuttering and bizarre nervous laughter and smiling. Three subjects had uncontrollable seizures. The teacher-volunteers who continued the shock frequently voiced their concern for the learner-victim, but the majority overcame their humane reactions and continued as ordered right up to the maximum punishment.

One observer related: 'I observed a mature and initially poised businessman enter the laboratory smiling and confident. Within 20 minutes he was reduced to a twitching, stuttering wreck, who was rapidly approaching a point of nervous collapse. He constantly pulled on his earlobe and twisted his hands. At one point he pushed his fist into his forehead and muttered: "Oh God, let's stop it." And yet he continued to respond to every word of the experimenter, and obeyed to the end.'

The conflict that the subjects faced in this experiment was between obeying an authority they trusted and respected, and doing something they felt to be wrong. The real-life situation is more horrible. There is, for many, perhaps no conflict at all. My guess is that *most* people feel guilty at *not* doing what they are told, even though they think it is wrong, and even though they mistrust those who give the orders. They feel guilty at trusting their own mistrust.

It would be nice to live in a world where we could feel that if one of the authorities of society – whether Mao, the Pope, or Lyndon Johnson, and their acolytes – told us something, the fact that they said so would make it more likely to be true than false. It would be nice, even, if one could believe that something that appears in any of our journals of scholarship, or medical or social-science research, was more likely to be true than false by the fact of its publication. Unfortunately we are forced by the cynical lies, multifarious deceptions and sincerely held delusions to which we are now subjected through all media – even the organs of scholarship and science – to a position of almost total social scepticism. There is almost nothing we *can* know about the total social world system, or any of the systems for several levels down from there. But it is possible to know that we cannot so know – this being a historical contingency of the present world situation, but given that situation, a necessity of that situation. Yet we are so 'programmed' to believe that what we are told is more likely to be true than false because we are told it, that almost all of us are liable to be caught out occasionally. We have all a 'reflex' towards believing and doing what we are told.

We can put no trust in princes, popes, politicians, scholars or scientists, our worst enemy or our best friend. With the greatest precautions, we may put trust in a source that is much deeper than our egos – if we can trust ourselves to have found it, or rather, to have been found by it. It is obvious that it is hidden, but what it is and where it is, is not obvious.

References

1. *Contemporary China,* ed. Ruth Adams, Vintage Books, N.Y., 1966, p. viii.
2. See *The Bitter Heritage. Vietnam and American Democracy, 1941–1966,* Arthur M. Schlesinger Jnr, Sphere Books, London, 1967. Schlesinger's position is all the more interesting as he has been so much a part of the administrative élite.
3. See *Air War: Vietnam,* Frank Harvey, Bantam, London, 1967.
4. 'Mirror Role of Mother and Family in Child Development', (1967). D. W. Winnicott, in *The Predicament of the Family,* ed Peter Lomas. Hogarth Press, London.
5. As summarized in: *New York Academy of Science,* 4, 4 18–20, 1964. Milgram's original paper is: 'Behavioural Study of Obedience'. (1963) *Journal of Abnormal and Social Psychology.* 67, p. 371–9.

Conscious Purpose Versus Nature | *Gregory Bateson*

Our civilization, which is on the block here for investigation and evaluation, has its roots in three main ancient civilizations: the Roman, the Hebrew and the Greek; and it would seem that many of our problems are related to the fact that we have an imperialist civilization leavened or yeasted by a downtrodden, exploited colony in Palestine. In this conference, we are again going to be fighting out the conflict between the Romans and the Palestinians.

You will remember that St Paul boasted, 'I was born free'. What he meant was that he was born Roman, and that this had certain legal advantages.

We can engage in that old battle either by backing the downtrodden or by backing the imperialists. If you are going to fight that battle, you have to take sides in it. It's that simple.

On the other hand, of course, St Paul's ambition, and the ambition of the downtrodden, is always to get on the side of the imperialists – to become middle-class imperialists themselves – and it is doubtful whether creating more members of the civilization which we are here criticizing is a solution to the problem.

There is, therefore, another more abstract problem. We need to understand the pathologies and peculiarities of the whole Romano-Palestinian system. It is this that I am interested in talking about. I do not care, here, about defending the Romans or defending the Palestinians – the upper dogs or the underdogs. I want to consider the dynamics of the whole traditional pathology in which we are caught, and in which we shall remain as long as we continue to struggle within that old conflict. We just go round and round in terms of the old premises.

Fortunately our civilization has a third root – in Greece. Of course Greece got caught up in a rather similar mess, but still there was a lot of clean, cool thinking of a quite surprising kind which was different.

Let me approach the bigger problem historically. From St Thomas Aquinas to the eighteenth century in Catholic countries, and to the Reformation among Protestants (because we threw out a lot of Greek sophistication with the Reformation), the structure of our religion was Greek. In mid-eighteenth century the biological world looked like this: There was a supreme mind at the top of the ladder, which was the basic explanation of everything downwards from that – the supreme mind being, in Christianity, God; and having various attributes at various philosophic stages. The ladder of explanation went downwards deductively from the Supreme to man to the apes, and so on, down to the infusoria.

This hierarchy was a set of deductive steps from the most perfect to the most crude or simple. And it was rigid. It was assumed that every species was unchanging.

Lamarck, probably the greatest biologist in history, turned that ladder of explanation upside down. He was the man who said it starts with the infusoria and that there were changes leading up to man, His turning the taxonomy upside down is one of the most astonishing feats that has ever occurred. It was the equivalent in biology of the Copernican revolution in astronomy.

The logical outcome of turning the taxonomy upside down was that the study of evolution might provide an explanation of *mind*.

Up to Lamarck, mind was the explanation of the biological world. But, hey presto, the question now arose: is the biological world the explanation of mind? That which was the explanation now became that which was to be explained. About three quarters of Lamarck's *Philosophie Zoologique* (1809) is an attempt, very crude, to build a comparative psychology. He achieved and formulated a number of very modern ideas: that you cannot attribute to any creature psychological capacities for which it has no organs; that mental process must always have physical representation; and that the complexity of the nervous system is related to the complexity of mind.

There the matter rested for 150 years, mainly because evolutionary theory was taken over, not by a Catholic heresy but by a Protestant heresy, in the mid-nineteenth century. Darwin's opponents, you may remember, were not Aristotle and Aquinas, who had some sophistication, but fundamentalist Christians whose sophistication stopped with the first chapter of Genesis. The question of the nature of mind was something which the nineteenth-century evolutionists tried to exclude from their theories, and the matter did not come up again for serious consideration until after World War II. (I am doing some injustice to some heretics along the road, notably to Samuel Butler – and others.)

In World War II it was discovered what sort of complexity entails mind. And, since that discovery, we know that: wherever in the Universe we encounter that sort of complexity, we are dealing with mental phenomena. It's as materialistic as that.

Let me try to describe for you that order of complexity, which is in some degree a technical matter. Russel Wallace sent a famous essay to Darwin from Indonesia. In it he announced his discovery of natural selection, which coincided with Darwin's. Part of his description of the struggle for existence is interesting:

The action of this principle [the struggle for existence] is exactly like that of the steam engine, which checks and corrects any irregularities almost before they become evident; and in like manner no unbalanced deficiency in the animal kingdom can ever reach any conspicuous magnitude, because it would make itself felt at the very first step, by rendering existence difficult and extinction almost sure to follow.

The steam engine with a governor is simply a circular train of causal events, with somewhere a link in that chain such that the more of something, the less of the next thing in the circuit. The *wider* the balls of the governor diverge, the *less* the fuel supply. If causal chains with that general characteristic are provided with energy, the result will be (if you are lucky and things balance out) a self-corrective system.

Wallace, in fact, proposed the first cybernetic model.

Nowadays cybernetics deal with much more complex systems of this general kind; and we know that when we talk about the processes of civilization, or evaluating human behaviour, human organization, or any biological system, we are concerned with self-corrective systems. Basically these systems are always *conservative* of something. As in the engine with a governor, the fuel supply is changed to conserve – to keep constant – the speed of the flywheel, so always in such systems changes occur to conserve the truth of some descriptive statement, some component of the *status quo*. Wallace saw the matter correctly, and natural selection acts primarily to keep the species unvarying; but it may act at higher levels to keep constant that complex variable which we call 'survival'.

Dr Laing noted that the obvious can be very difficult for people to see. That is because people are self-corrective systems. They are self-corrective against disturbance, and if the obvious is not a kind that they can easily assimilate without internal disturbance, their self-corrective mechanisms work to side-track it, to hide it, even to the extent of shutting the eyes if necessary, or shutting off various parts of the process of perception. Disturbing information can be framed like a pearl so that it doesn't make a nuisance of itself; and this will be done, according to the understanding of the system itself of what would be a nuisance. This too – the premise regarding what would cause disturbance – is something which is learned and then becomes perpetuated or conserved.

At this conference, fundamentally, we deal with three of these enormously complex systems or arrangements of conservative loops. One is the human individual. Its physiology and neurology conserve body temperature, blood chemistry, the length and size and shape of organs during growth and embryology, and all the rest of the body's characteristics. This is a system which conserves descriptive statements about the human being, body or soul. For the same is true of the psychology of the individual, where learning occurs to conserve the opinions and components of the *status quo*.

Second, we deal with the society in which that individual lives – and that society is again a system of the same general kind.

And third, we deal with the ecosystem, the natural biological surroundings of these human animals.

Let me start from the natural ecosystems around man. An English oak wood, or a tropical forest, or a piece of desert, is a community of creatures. In the oak wood perhaps 1,000 species, perhaps more; in the tropical forest perhaps ten times that number of species live together.

I may say that very few of you here have ever seen such an undisturbed system; there are not many of them left; they've mostly been messed up by *Homo sapiens* who either exterminated some species or introduced others which became weeds and pests, or altered the water supply, etc., etc. We are rapidly, of course, destroying all the natural systems in the world, the balanced natural systems. We simply make them unbalanced – but still natural.

Be that as it may, those creatures and plants live together

in a combination of competition and mutual dependency, and it is that combination that is the important thing to consider. Every species has a primary Malthusian capacity. Any species that does not, potentially, produce more young than the number of the population of the parental generation is out. They're doomed. It is absolutely necessary for every species and for every such system that its components have a potential positive gain in the population curve. But, if every species has potential gain, it is then quite a trick to achieve equilibrium. All sorts of interactive balances and dependencies come into play, and it is these processes that have the sort of circuit-structure that I have mentioned.

The Malthusian curve is exponential. It is the curve of population growth and it is not inappropriate to call this the population *explosion*.

You may regret that organisms have this explosive characteristic, but you may as well settle for it. The creatures that don't are out.

On the other hand, in a balanced ecological system whose underpinnings are of this nature, it is very clear that any monkeying with the system is likely to disrupt the equilibrium. Then the exponential curves will start to appear. Some plant will become a weed, some creatures will be exterminated, and the system as a *balanced* system is likely to fall to pieces.

What is true of the species that live together in a wood is also true of the groupings and sorts of people in a society, who are similarly in an uneasy balance of dependency and competition. And the same truth holds right inside you, where there is an uneasy physiological competition and mutual dependency among the organs, tissues, cells and so on. Without this competition and dependency you would not be, because you cannot do without any of the competing organs and parts. If any of the parts did not have the expansive characteristics they would go out, and you would go out too. So that even in the body you have a liability. With improper disturbance of the system, the exponential curves appear.

In a society, the same is true.

I think you have to assume that all important physiological or social change is in some degree a slipping of the system at some point along an exponential curve. The slippage may not go far, or it may go to disaster. But in principle if, say, you kill off the thrushes in a wood, certain components of the balance will run along exponential curves to a new stopping place.

In such slippage there is always danger – the possibility that some variable, e.g. population density, may reach such a value that further slippage is controlled by factors which are inherently harmful. If, for example, population is finally controlled by available food supply, the surviving individuals will be half starved and the food supply over-grazed, usually to a point of no return.

Now let me begin to talk about the individual organism. This entity is similar to the oak wood and its controls are represented in the *total* mind, which is perhaps only a reflection of the total body. But the system is segmented in various ways, so that the effects of something in your food-life, shall we say, do not totally alter your sex-life, and things in your sex-life do not totally change your kinesic life, and so on. There is a certain amount of compartmentalization, which is no doubt a necessary economy. There is one compartmentalization which is in many ways mysterious but certainly of crucial importance in man's life. I refer to the 'semi-permeable' linkage between consciousness and the remainder of the total mind. A certain limited amount of information about what's happening in this larger part of the mind seems to be relayed to what we may call the screen of consciousness. But what gets to consciousness is selected; it is a systematic (not random) sampling of the rest.

Of course, the *whole* of the mind could not be reported in a *part* of the mind. This follows logically from the relationship between part and whole. The television screen does not give you total coverage or report of the events which occur in the whole television process; and this not merely because the viewers would not be interested in such a report, but because to report on any extra part of the total process would require extra circuitry. But to report on the events in this extra circuitry would require a still further addition of more circuitry, and so on. Each additional step towards increased consciousness will take the system farther from total consciousness. To add a report on events in a given part of the machine will actually *decrease* the percentage of total events reported.

We therefore have to settle for very limited consciousness, and the question arises: How is the selecting done? On what principles does your mind select that which 'you' will be aware of? And, while not much is known of these principles, something is known, though the principles at work are often not themselves accessible to consciousness. First of all, much of the input is consciously scanned, but only *after* it has been processed by the totally unconscious process of perception. The sensory events are packaged into images and these images are then 'conscious'.

I, the conscious I, see an unconsciously edited version of a small percentage of what affects my retina. I am guided in my perception by *purposes*. I see who is attending, who is not, who is understanding, who is not, or at least I get a myth about this subject, which may be quite correct. I am interested in getting that myth as I talk. It is relevant to my purposes that you hear me.

What happens to the picture of a cybernetic system – an oak wood or an organism – when that picture is selectively drawn to answer only questions of purpose?

Consider the state of medicine today. It's called medical

science. What happens is that doctors think it would be nice to get rid of polio, or typhoid, or cancer. So they devote research money and effort to focusing on these 'problems', or purposes. At a certain point Dr Salk and others 'solve' the problem of polio. They discover a solution of bugs which you can give to children so that they don't get polio. This is the solution to the problem of polio. At this point, they stop putting large quantities of effort and money into the problem of polio and go on to the problem of cancer, or whatever it may be.

Medicine ends up, therefore, as a total science, whose structure is essentially that of a bag of tricks. Within this science there is extraordinarily little knowledge of the sort of things I'm talking about; that is, of the body as a systemically cybernetically organized self-corrective system. Its internal interdependencies are minimally understood. What has happened is that *purpose* has determined what will come under the inspection or consciousness of medical science.

If you allow purpose to organize that which comes under your conscious inspection, what you will get is a bag of tricks – some of them very valuable tricks. It is an extraordinary achievement that these tricks have been discovered; all that I don't argue. But still we do not know two-penn'orth, really, about the total network system. Cannon wrote a book on *The Wisdom of the Body*, but nobody has written a book on the wisdom of medical science, because wisdom is precisely the thing which it lacks. Wisdom I take to be the knowledge of the larger interactive system – that system which, if disturbed, is likely to generate exponential curves of change.

Consciousness operates in the same way as medicine in its sampling of the events and processes of the body and of what goes on in the total mind. It is organized in terms of purpose. It is a short-cut device to enable you to get quickly at what you want; not to act with maximum wisdom in order to live, but to follow the shortest logical or causal path to get what you next want, which may be dinner; it may be a Beethoven sonata; it may be sex. Above all, it may be money or power.

But you may say: 'Yes, but we have lived that way for a million years.' Consciousness and purpose have been characteristic of man for at least a million years, and may have been with us a great deal longer than that. I am not prepared to say that dogs and cats are not conscious, still less that porpoises are not conscious.

So you may say: 'Why worry about that?'

But what worries me is the addition of modern technology to the old system. Today the purposes of consciousness are implemented by more and more effective machinery, transportation systems, airplanes, weaponry, medicine, pesticides and so forth. Conscious purpose is now empowered to upset the balances of the body, of society and of the biological world around us. A pathology – a loss of balance – is threatened.

I think that much of what brings us here today is basically related to the thoughts that I have been putting before you. On the one hand, we have the systemic nature of the individual human being, the systemic nature of the culture in which he lives, and the systemic nature of the biological, ecological system around him; and, on the other hand, the curious twist in the systemic nature of the individual man whereby consciousness is, almost of necessity, blinded to the systemic nature of the man himself. Purposive consciousness pulls out, from the total mind, sequences which do not have the loop-structure which is characteristic of the whole systemic structure. If you follow the 'commonsense' dictates of consciousness you become, effectively, greedy and unwise – again I use 'wisdom' as a word for recognition of and guidance by a knowledge of the total systemic creature.

Lack of systemic wisdom is always punished. We may say that the biological systems – the individual, the culture and the ecology – are partly living sustainers of their component cells or organisms. But the systems are none the less punishing of any species unwise enough to quarrel with its ecology. Call the systemic forces 'God' if you will.

Let me offer you a myth.

There was once a Garden. It contained many hundreds of species – probably in the sub-tropics – living in great fertility and balance, with plenty of humus, and so on. In that garden, there were two anthropoids who were more intelligent than the other animals.

On one of the trees there was a fruit, very high up, which the two apes were unable to reach. So they began to *think*. That was the mistake. They began to think purposively.

By and by, the he ape, whose name was Adam, went and got an empty box and put it under the tree and stepped on it, but he found he still couldn't reach the fruit. So he got another box and put it on top of the first. Then he climbed up on the two boxes and finally he got that apple.

Adam and Eve then became almost drunk with excitement. *This* was the way to do things. Make a plan, A B C and you get D.

They then began to specialize in doing things the planned way. In effect, they cast out from the Garden the concept of their own total systemic nature and of its total systemic nature.

After they had cast God out of the Garden, they really went to work on this purposive business, and pretty soon the topsoil disappeared. After that, several species of plants became 'weeds' and some of the animals became 'pests'; and Adam found that gardening was much harder work. He had to get his bread by the sweat of his brow and he said, 'It's a vengeful God. I should never have eaten that apple'.

Moreover, there occurred a qualitative change in the relationship between Adam and Eve, after they had discarded God from the Garden. Eve began to resent the business of sex and reproduction. Whenever these rather basic phenomena intruded upon her now purposive way of living, she was reminded of the larger life which had been kicked out of the Garden. So Eve began to resent sex and reproduction, and when it came to parturition she found this process very painful. She said this too was due to the vengeful nature of God. She even heard a Voice say 'in pain shalt thou bring forth' and 'thy desire shall be unto thy husband, and he shall rule over thee'.

The biblical version of this story, from which I have borrowed extensively, does not explain the extraordinary perversion of values, whereby the woman's capacity for love comes to seem a curse inflicted by the deity.

Be that as it may. Adam went on pursuing his purposes and finally invented the free-enterprise system. Eve was not, for a long time, allowed to participate in this because she was a woman. But she joined a bridge club and there found an outlet for her hate.

In the next generation, they again had trouble with love. Cain, the inventor and innovator, was told by God that 'his [Abel's] desire shall be unto thee and thou shalt rule over him'. So he killed Abel.

A parable, of course, is not data about human behaviour. It is only an explanatory device. But I have built into it a phenomenon which seems to be almost universal when man commits the error of purposive thinking and disregards the systemic nature of the world with which he must deal. This phenomenon is called by the psychologists 'projection'. The man, after all, has acted according to what he thought was common sense and now he finds himself in a mess. He does not quite know what caused the mess and he feels that what has happened is somehow unfair. He still does not see himself as part of the system in which the mess exists, and he either blames the rest of the system or he blames himself. In my parable Adam combines two sorts of nonsense: the notion 'I have sinned' and the notion 'God is vengeful'.

If you look at the real situations in our world where the systemic nature of the world has been ignored in favour of purpose or common sense, you will find a rather similar reaction. President Johnson is, no doubt, fully aware that he has a mess on his hands, not only in Vietnam but in other parts of the national and international ecosystems; and I am sure that from where he sits it appears that he followed his purposes with common sense and that the mess must be due either to the wickedness of others or to his own sin or to some combination of these, according to his temperament.

And the terrible thing about such situations is that inevitably they shorten the time span of all planning. Emergency is present or only just around the corner; and long-term wisdom must therefore be sacrificed to expediency, even though there is a dim awareness that expediency will never give a long-term solution.

Morever, since we are engaged in diagnosing the machinery of our own society, let me add one point: Our politicians – both those in a state of power and those in a state of protest or hunger for power – are alike utterly ignorant of the matters which I have been discussing. You can search the Congressional Record for speeches which show awareness that the problems of government are biological problems, and you will find very, very few that apply biological insight. Extraordinary!

In general, governmental decisions are made by persons who are as ignorant of these matters as pigeons. Like the famous Dr Skinner, in *The Way of All Flesh*, they 'combine the wisdom of the dove with the harmlessness of the serpent'.

But we are met here not only for diagnosis of some of the world's ills but also to think about remedies. I have already suggested that no simple remedy to what I called the Romano-Palestinian problem can be achieved by backing the Romans against the Palestinians or *vice versa*. The problem is systemic and the solution must surely depend upon realizing this fact.

First, there is humility, and I propose this not as a moral principle, distasteful to a large number of people, but simply as an item of a scientific philosophy. In the period of the Industrial Revolution, perhaps the most important disaster was the enormous increase of scientific arrogance. We had discovered how to make trains and other machines. We knew how to put one box on top of the other to get that apple, and occidental man saw himself as an autocrat with complete power over a universe which was made of physics and chemistry. And the biological phenomena were in the end to be controlled like processes in a test tube. Evolution was the history of how organisms learned more tricks for controlling the environment; and man had better tricks than any other creature.

But that arrogant scientific philosophy is now obsolete and in its place there is the discovery that man is only a part of larger systems and that the part can never control the whole.

Goebbels thought that he could control public opinion in Germany with a vast communication system and our own public-relations men are perhaps liable to similar delusions. But in fact the would-be controller must always have his spies out to tell him what the people are saying about his propaganda. He is therefore in the position of being *responsive* to what they are saying. Therefore he cannot have a simple lineal control. We do not live in the sort of universe in which simple lineal control is possible. Life is not like that.

Similarly, in the field of psychiatry, the family is a cybernetic system of the sort which I am discussing and usually when systemic pathology occurs, the members blame each other, or sometimes themselves. But the truth of the matter is that both these alternatives are fundamentally arrogant. Either alternative assumes that the individual human being has total power over the system of which he or she is a part.

Even within the individual human being, control is limited. We can in some degree set ourselves to learn even such abstract characteristics as arrogance or humility, but we are not by any means the captains of our souls.

It is, however, possible that the remedy for ills of conscious purpose lies with the individual. There is what Freud called the royal road to the unconscious. He was referring to dreams, but I think we should lump together dreams and the creativity of art, or the perception of art, and poetry and such things. And I would include with these the best of religion. These are all activities in which the whole individual is involved. The artist may have a conscious purpose to sell his picture, even perhaps a conscious purpose to make it. But in the making he must necessarily relax that arrogance in favour of a creative experience in which his conscious mind plays only a small part.

We might say that in creative art man must experience himself – his total self – as a cybernetic model.

It is characteristic of the 1960s that a large number of people are looking to the psychedelic drugs for some sort of wisdom or some sort of enlargement of consciousness, and I think this symptom of our epoch probably arises as an attempt to compensate for our excessive purposiveness. But I am not sure that wisdom can be got that way. What is required is not simply a relaxation of consciousness to let the unconscious material gush out. To do this is merely to exchange one partial view of the self for the other partial view. I suspect that what is needed is the synthesis of the two views and this is more difficult.

My own slight experience of LSD led me to believe that Prospero was wrong when he said, 'We are such stuff as dreams are made on'. It seemed to me that pure dream was, like pure purpose, rather trivial. It was not the stuff of which we are made, but only bits and pieces of that stuff. Our conscious purposes, similarly, are only bits and pieces.

The systemic view is something else again.

Social and Psychological Preparation
for War | *Jules Henry*

War is fought by social groups. Social groups exist in a mobilized and unmobilized condition. For the conduct of everyday affairs social groups are integrated, tied together, by processes which, ranging from the simple exchange of commodities and services of tribal peoples, to the interlocking corporations, fiscal obligations and controls and industry-government relations in modern states, provide continuity and dependability. Mobilized, such groups are prepared for extra effort, for an output greater than the requirements of everyday life. In time of war latent capabilities for action are actualized, with the aid of the society's capacity for love, hate and anxiety.

DEFINING THE ENEMY. The 'enemy', however, is, himself, an aspect or mode of the dialectics of the organization of the society. In the tribal world, for example, where, as compared with the modern world, each society is relatively self-contained, the 'enemy' is usually outside the social system.*

In the modern world, however, the enemy is, by definition, and by dialectic necessity, a part, but also not a part, of the 'friendly' social configuration that acts against it in war. In modern states the 'enemy' is linked to one's own social system by trade, by various cultural ties, by diplomatic relations, and so on, as well as by destructive chains of impulses and activities. The initial bellicose step of 'break-

*The Indian tribes of eastern South America constitute an outstanding exception to this generalization. For one example see *Jungle People*, Random House, Vintage Books, 1965 (first published in 1941).

ing relations' testifies to this ambiguity. The requirement in modern warfare that the enemy usually be part of the social system of the contending countries and, at the same time, not part, is one of the social inventions of modern civilization, for if one goes back to ancient histories one perceives that ancient wars were often, though not always, fought against enemies not part of one's social system. The enemies of ancient Greece and Rome were often mere objects of their imperial arrogance and rapine, having no previous social relations with Greece and Rome. Thus one of the 'achievements' of the modern world is to incorporate war directly into the social system, while defining the enemy as outside it. The net consequence of this, for the United States, has been sundry Marshall Plans, foreign aid programmes, economic development plans for South-east Asia, and the like. These programmes recognize the essentially *internal* nature of modern war and modern enemies. The post-war 'compassion' of the modern 'victor', which recognizes the basic unity of the world social system, and therefore dresses the enemy's wounds, is at 180 degrees from those ancient wars, in which the defeated enemy was put to the sword, enslaved, or condemned to tribute. This modern 'compassion' is partly a consequence of interlocking international corporations, partly an expression of the need to use one's former enemies against one's former friends. America's use of Japan – particularly of Okinawa – as a staging area and source of supply for the war in Vietnam, and her support of German claims and hopes against the Soviet Union, are cases in point.

A basic fact of modern warfare, then, is that it occurs within a mutually dependent world political economy and that all victories are therefore defeats for the people – for they have borne the burden of death and, through taxation, must bear the economic burden of compassion – and victories for the vanquished, for they often see their economies

beautifully reconstructed. Japan is an excellent case in point.*
Nowadays Japanese capital competes with American almost
everywhere in the world, Japan is almost as deeply involved
as the United States in Canada, and Japan has heavy investments in Alaska. Indeed, Japan's economic fate is so closely
linked to that of the United States that on 9 February
1967, when rumours of peace in Vietnam broke out, prices
for 225 selected stocks on the Tokyo market dropped an
average of 42.12 points, the worst setback since 19 July
1963.†

To continue with the example of Japan, business and technological know-how combined with low wages have given
Japan such economic power that U.S. involvement in South-
east Asia is aimed as much at monopolizing that market
against Japanese penetration as against Chinese. The Vietnam war is indirectly a war against Japan, who is part of our
social system, and whom, at the same time, the U.S. is using
in order to further her ends in Asia.

Not all wars are shooting wars or even cold ones. For
years the United States has been fighting a kind of cold
war with France, and England is a kind of casualty of that
war. France's (largely unsuccessful) efforts to keep American capital out, its determination to build its own computer
industry and nuclear capability, its efforts to diminish
American gold paramountcy and its objection to Britain's
entrance into the Common Market are all expressions, in
part, of fear of United States' economic power.

It is clear, therefore, that in preparation for modern war
an interdependent world political economy has within it
sufficient conflicts of interest to make all nations potential
enemies to all others. One of the 'evolutionary achieve-

---

* Japan's gross national product in the 1960s is many times what
it was before World War II. See *Newsweek: Economic Almanac
1964* and *Japan: Statistical Yearbook 1965*.

† *N.Y. Times,* 2 October 1967.

ments' of modern culture has been to make the idea that 'anybody can be my enemy at any time' acceptable. A consequence of the definition of the enemy as part of one's own social system is a psychological predisposition to accept almost any nation at all as inimical when the government chooses to so define it.

The absolute division of the world into communist and non-communist nations multiplies the probability of enemies. Here we must ask, who divides the world into communist and non-communist? and the answer is, of course, those who stand to gain by it. Obviously John Doe did not make the division; and obviously the example of Western Europe in 1967 suggests that the *perception* of that division as rigidly constituting the *essence* of the modern world is not universal. Though it is true that the countries of Eastern Europe are roughly 'communist', they have different forms of it, and Yugoslavia could hardly be called communist at all. Meanwhile, however, the *perception* of these nations by others varies also, so that though Americans see them all as inimical, Europeans perceive them less nightmarishly. The point at issue is that the social organization of the world has no essence. The delusion that is made to appear as essence is manufactured by those who stand to gain by it and it is burned into the minds of the population by the media, which are, of course, controlled by the same people. This delusion then takes on the character of a true perception of the world, seeming as absolute to the average man as the difference between red and green.

In the United States the world is simplistically perceived by most people as made up of communist and 'free' nations, and all the former are perceived as enemy – as the enemies of 'freedom'. This simplistic definition of the world, however, is not accepted by much of Western Europe and the United Kingdom. The definition is thus a parochial American one, based on the interests of those who foster it. If the French do not perceive the world as Americans do, it is because French interests have nothing to gain by it but much to lose. The condition of West Germany, meanwhile, is absurd because, on the one hand, corporate interests there have everything to gain by forgetting the 'communist–Free world' definition, while on the other, no West German government could risk American pressure or a victory of the extreme right by seeming to cancel the old feud with the Soviet Union. American interests can only be furthered by German hankerings after old borders, for they help maintain the USSR in a state of expensive alert.

NO OPTIONS. The present situation in the Near East makes it clear that the organization of the world offers mankind limited options. When we consider that *shalom*, peace, is the word with which ordinary Israelis greet one another, that they are a people who know, better than most, what war means and that only through toil and peace have they been able to create a home, their war with the Arab states seems a contradiction. Yet the configuration of the world society, of which they are part, and the fact that the world system defined them as another enemy within, drove them to war. The social structure of the modern world has so limited the possibilities of existence that even emerging nations from which we might expect some new ideas, some new salvation, are forced into the old ways of predator and prey. North Vietnam and the Congo are further examples of emerging nations forced into an old pattern. The present world political economy leaves mankind almost no room to exploit or to think about new ways of political existence. This means that under the present system man has no choice but to make war upon himself.

The social preparation for modern war therefore involves the following steps: (1) Establishment of a world system in which betrayal, conspiracy and entrapment are so commonplace that at any moment whoever is within the friendly system may be defined as outside of it; so commonplace, indeed, that people accept it without thinking. (2) Manipulation of that system in the interests of particular classes or groups who stand to gain by particular definitions. (3) The manipulation, the moulding of the perceptual capacities of the people by these groups through their control of the mass media. (4) The establishment of a world-wide social system which strictly limits choice. In this context Charles de Gaulle's efforts to free France of American economic entanglements represent not only an effort to be free of the United States as such, but also an effort to be free of limiting options; to be free to seek new solutions to the problems of a hampering social system; and in this context English economic entanglement with the United States illustrates the impossibility of ever arriving at new solutions to one's problems as long as one is committed to a powerful ally who sees only the old, and limited, possibilities. The same holds within the group of states allied to the USSR. I hope I am making myself clear. All social systems have been set up in such a way as to limit options. Whether it be a primitive tribe where a man must marry his mother's brother's daughter and cultivate his land with the help of his clan brothers only; whether it be the members of the old British Commonwealth, trading largely with those within the sterling area; or whether it be the United States Government trying to stop the sale by other nations of so-called strategic materials to the 'communist' nations, every society, throughout history, has buttressed its internal structure and mobilized against outsiders by limiting choice. Fundamentally, primordially, free choice has been viewed as inimical to any social system. Arguments about free choice, therefore, have been absurd when they have not been hypocritical.

The American economy

I turn now to an analysis of the organization of the American economy: In order to show how readily it can be mobilized for anything at all.

In order that any social system be mobilized for war, which means mobilization for maximum effort, it must have forms of structure – institutions – which can swiftly be brought together and integrated into a war system when necessary. While it might appear 'only natural' that America should have been able to produce the implements of war that made victory over the Axis possible, the astonishing and rapid organization of that productive capability was not accomplished easily, nor was it accomplished just before or during World War II. The latent possibility for such organization existed long before World War II and the consolidation process was hastened by the immense insecurity of the Great Depression. 'The modern centralized, militarized, and welfare-directed state'* is the result of a complex internal evolution taking several decades. I shall trace the pattern.

CONCENTRATION AND SIZE. The ability of any social unit to wage war or, indeed, to exercise power in any way is a function of its size, of the resources it controls, and of its organization. In this connexion we have to understand something of the dimensions of the larger American corporations. In 1962 the four largest automobile manufacturers accounted for nearly 80 per cent of the automobile sales in the United States; the two largest steel companies for 30 per cent of the sales and the ten largest oil companies

* These are the words of Thomas C. Cochran in his book *The Business System,* Harvard University Press, 1960, p. vii. Dr Cochran is professor of American History at the University of Pennsylvania.

accounted for more than 85 per cent of the petroleum refining and related industry sales. Twenty-eight of the largest industrial and commercial companies accounted for almost a quarter of the sales of the manufacturing companies in the United States.*

The United States Steel Corporation, which in 1965 produced one quarter of the total steel output of the United States,† is an integrated corporation, which owns and operates not only numerous steel producing and fabricating plants, but also iron and coal mines, limestone quarries, railways, docks, cargo vessels and loading ships. Through several score plants in the United States it manufactures thousands of products, ranging from cold rolled steel to prefabricated housing, cement, ordinance, atomic energy products, components and launching facilities for nuclear missiles, armour plate, etc., etc., etc.‡ The size of the corporation, however, is not measured only by the plants directly connected with it, but includes also its seventeen subsidiaries through which it controls raw materials, railroads and other transportation facilities in Canada, Brazil, Venezuela, Africa, and the Bahama Islands. Through its management and board of directors the influence of U.S. Steel, meanwhile, extends far beyond its plants and subsidiaries. In 1962 its eighteen directors accounted for eighty-five management interlocks with other companies, over which these directors might be expected to exercise influence, and these interlocks included twenty banks and financial institutions, ten insurance companies and fifty-four industrial-commercial corporations. Thus Mr C. H. Bell, for example, was also a director of General Mills, Inc.,

*P. 115 of 'Interlocks in Corporate Management', a Staff Report on the Antitrust Subcommittee (Subcommittee Report No. 5) of the Committee on the Judiciary, US House of Representatives, 12 March 1965.

† Moody's Manual 1966, p. 2230.

‡ Moody's Manual 1966, pp. 2229–32.

the Winton Lumber Company, and the Northern Pacific Railway; and Mr J. B. Black sat on the board of directors of FMC corporation, Del Monte Properties Company, Pacific Gas and Electric Company, Southern Pacific Company, Shell Oil, Pacific Gas Transmission Company, Alberta Natural Gas Company, and the Alberta and Southern Gas Company Limited.*

The Dow Chemical Company,† manufacturer extraordinary of napalm and explosives, operates several dozen plants in the United States, but through subsidiaries and through part ownership it controls or is deeply involved in other scores of manufacturing operations and corporations in the United Kingdom (Dow Chemical International Ltd), Switzerland, the Netherlands, Germany, Australia, India and Spain. Through its affiliation with Schlumberger Ltd, Dow substantially controls plants in France, Germany, Spain, Spanish Sahara, Algeria, Libya, Tunisia, Iran, Venezuela, Trinidad, Bolivia and Argentina. Other operations substantially controlled by Dow are in Japan (Asahi-Dow Ltd) and Ecuador. Literally the sun never sets on Dow! Thus through sheer size, through subsidiaries, through ownership of stock in other corporations and through management interlocks, the large American corporations control much of the productive capability of the planet. In 1951, 135 American corporations *owned* nearly a fourth of the manufacturing volume of the world.‡ This says nothing about how much is *controlled*, how much is a sphere of interest, that is not owned outright.

* 'Interlocks . . .', pp. 126–8.
† *Moody's Manual 1966*, pp. 2804–5.
‡ 'The Measurement of Industrial Concentration' by M. A. Adelman, in *The Review of Economics and Statistics*, Vol. XXX, No. 2, 1951. Quoted in A. A. Berle Jr., *The 20th Century Capitalist Revolution*, Harcourt Brace (Harvest Books), 1954.

The presence of hundreds of corporations, which, in their day-to-day operations, can, through their social organization, call upon such an immensely ramifying network of productive power, provides the United States with a vast war potential.

INTEREST GROUPS. The internal organization of the companies themselves, plus their interlocks, does not of itself constitute the social organization of American corporate power. These great masses of capital are further organized in what has been called 'interest groups'.* The interest group is a group of corporate interests which, through interlocking directorates, mutual stock ownership, financial support, auditing and legal activities and membership in the same trade organizations, come to pursue common financial goals. If various companies share board members and own one another's stocks and bonds; if, further, certain financial institutions assume the burden of underwriting (financial responsibility) and disposing of stock flotations for certain corporations, while others consistently render legal and auditing services to all, we have a common financial interest and, therefore, a common-interest group. *The Structure of the American Economy* lists *eight* such groups: (1) The Morgan-First National, (2) Rockefeller, (3) Kuhn, Loeb, (4) Mellon, (5) Chicago, (6) Du Pont, (7) Cleveland, (8) Boston.

I present an abbreviated account of one such group, the Morgan-First National, as it stood on the last date for which we have adequate information. *The Structure of the American Economy* states that

This group is for the most part based upon partial control by one

* In *The Structure of the American Economy*, US Government Printing Office, 1939. While some of the data in this great book are out of date, the main features of the analysis remain substantially correct.

or the other, or, more commonly, by both of the financial institutions (i.e J.P. Morgan & Company and The First National Bank) after which the group is named. This partial control is based upon long-standing financial relations and the very great prestige attaching to the Morgan and First National firms ...

When that passage was written, the group included thirteen industrial corporations, thirteen public utilities corporations, six railway systems and three banks besides Morgan and First National. In 1939 their total assets were more than thirty billion dollars.

But this is not the end of this pyramiding of power, for the inter-relationships among the interest groups themselves result in further concentrations and integration. Thus there are close relations, through interlocking directorates, underwriting, mutual stock ownership and so on, between Morgan-First National and Mellon; between Morgan-First National and Chicago; between Kuhn, Loeb and Cleveland, and so on. Altogether, from the eight basic interest groups there emerge eleven overlaps. At the end of their analysis of interest groups, the authors of *The Structure of the American Economy* ask the following questions, which they do not answer:

What is the significance of the existence of more or less closely integrated interest groups for the pricing process? What are its implications for the relation between economic and political activity? How and to what extent do the views of leaders in the economic sphere make themselves felt in the life of the community?

These questions were not put by Marxists, for the committee that prepared the study was made up of six members of President Franklin D. Roosevelt's cabinet and four experts highly placed in American government and business. At any rate, it is clear that this is an organization 'in being', which, once mobilized by government, can exert irresistible power for war – or for peace. *It has never been mobilized for peace.*

The structure of *corporate* controls in the American economy has been set forth. What is still missing, what still remains to be elucidated is what makes it possible for government to use this organization for its own purposes when necessary; or, rather, for them to use each other.

RELATIONSHIPS BETWEEN GOVERNMENT AND BUSINESS. The most important relationship between business and government in the United States, or, rather, the reliance of the corporate community on government, began to take its present form during the Great Depression. Previously it was believed that the capitalist system was self-regulating, and this view, voiced by economists, was parroted, with certain avian embroidery of intonation and syllable, by famous sociologists like Pareto in Italy and by Talcott Parsons, Professor of Sociology at Harvard University in the United States. It is important to bear in mind the connexions between the illusions of the economists and those of the sociologists. Before the Great Depression nearly overturned the capitalist system in the United States, it was believed that depressions were, somehow, an expression of the inexorable operation of an eternal system, and that depressions always worked themselves out spontaneously. Depressions, it was believed, were nature's way of eliminating inefficient and weak firms, while leaving the field to strong, 'parent', companies, able to beget powerful offspring. The Depression, however, saw so many of the strong fail and threatened so many of the strongest, as month after month, year after year, the economy did not recover, while more and more businesses failed, that the corporate community was happy to seize the hand of government when it was extended in help. It was this *vulnerability* that created the new 'government-underwritten society' in the United States; but which also served to mobilize the United States better than ever for war. It was primarily the threat of internal collapse that perfected the underlying structure of mobilization for war; and it is clear that without such mobilization the economy would have collapsed. As late as 1940, when the United States was starting to arm, a conservative estimate of the number of unemployed in the American labour force was 13 per cent, but by 1944 they had all been put to work and the total number of employed workers had increased by 35 per cent.* During the Depression, however, new legislation enabled labour to organize at a tremendous rate and World War II gave the American workers an unprecedented rise in living standard. Organized labour was brought into wartime government, and the Office of Production Management was headed jointly by William S. Knudsen of General Motors and Sidney Hillman of the Amalgamated Clothing Workers, a powerful, but rather conservative member of the CIO. The experience of World War II was not lost on the American labour movement: war meant jobs, plenty of money and good times. Today organized labour in the United States is an active supporter of the war in Vietnam; and it is among the most virulent internal antagonists of the Soviet Union.

INDUSTRY AND THE MILITARY. Since 1939 immense US Government expenditures for armaments, and, more recently, for space exploration, have increased the power of the great corporations and created many new businesses. The aircraft industry is largely dependent on orders for military aircraft. The entrance of numerous business executives into government service during World War II consolidated the intimate relationship between government and business. But the end of the consolidation was not yet in sight. What was needed was a marriage of the military to

* *The American Business System*, p. 134.

industry. Considering the fact that most of the national budget of the United States now goes for military purposes, it was only natural that upon leaving the armed forces, or the Department of Defense, military men should be eagerly sought as employees by business.

In July 1960 . . . General Dynamics, the corporation having the largest per cent of armaments contracts (by dollars), had 27 retired generals and admirals on its payrolls. The *total* number of retired officers of all ranks employed by General Dynamics, however, was about 200. Its closest competitor was United Aircraft, with 171.*

All figures are probably low estimates. Meanwhile, we should not forget, of course, that Mr Robert McNamara, former president of the Ford Motor Company, is our Secretary of Defense and that an earlier one was Charles Wilson, President of General Motors.

I have outlined the organization of American industry that provides the social infra-structure for war. I have shown that the basis is, in the first place, the giant corporation with its ramifying network of plants, subsidiaries, and stockholdings that extend its influence throughout the nation and the world. I then pointed out how these corporations are linked to one another and organized into interest groups which are interlocked among themselves. I then described the process whereby the American corporate community, abandoning for ever the cry against government interference, became amalgamated with government, and I pointed out how the military has become part and parcel of American business. Given this structure, the traditional division of our society into business, government and military seems obsolete and illusory. Given this structure it is possible to mobilize American industry for war output almost instantaneously. It is not far-fetched to say that now, *by its very nature it is in a constant state of mobilization for war.*

* Quoted from my *Culture Against Man*, p. 105, fn.

Psychological factors

VULNERABILITY. While it is true that in all ages man has felt vulnerable, it is worth while to examine certain of the aspects of the feeling of vulnerability in the United States in order to understand how it contributes to readiness for war. I have pointed out that before the Great Depression it was assumed that the capitalist economy was self-regulating but that the depression experience destroyed that idea for ever in the minds of even the most bumptious economists, so that now all the 'talented' men of capitalist economies take the Keynesian theory of necessary government economic intervention for granted and instantly propose government measures whenever the economy seems to falter – which is now several times a year. The ordinary American, however, does not yet feel that the economy is to be trusted, for it has an unpredictable way of raising prices on him, throwing him out of a job or making his little investments and speculations vanish. The feeling of vulnerability in the United States is intensified by the increase in the number and power of socialist countries and by the fact that since the government-business-military complex cannot accept this as a tolerable fact of existence, they frighten the people.

The emergence since 1917 of this new socialist humanity has been accompanied by the disappearance or weakening of many capitalist powers, to the degree that, feeling beleaguered amidst the diminished strength of the capitalist world, America, according to Secretary of Defense Robert McNamara, 'has devoted a higher proportion of its gross national product to its military establishment than any other free-world nation. This was true even before the increased expenditures in Southeast Asia.

'We have had, over the last few years, as many men in uniform as all the nations of Western Europe combined – even though they have a population half again greater than our own.'* The rise of socialism and the doubling of the number of violent revolutions since 1958 (also according to Mr McNamara) left the American corporate community feeling so vulnerable that it eagerly and successfully communicated its fear and hate to the American people through the mass media. The result has been, as everyone knows, a supine Congress and a public that gives support to whatever the American government desires to do any place in the world.

TERROR AND EUPHORIA. In the economic view there are, fundamentally, two types of consumption, consumption in the private and consumption in the public sectors of the economy. Consumption in the private sector refers to egoistic things – all that a person buys to make living possible and enjoyable – but extending also to business expenditures; while consumption in the public sector refers to things like roads, schools, armaments and so on, on which government spends money. All governments have to calculate how much can be exacted in taxes for consumption in the public sector, while the need for the taxes is sold to the people by a combination of public relations, scaring and coercion. Taxes to support the war in Vietnam are exacted through scaring Americans with communism. Although taxes for government expenditures compete with spending for egoistic satisfactions, the American system of taxation converts exactions for public expenditures into egoistic consumption because taxes return to the consumer through the higher wages, higher employment and elevated standard of living that result from the pouring of hundreds of billions of dollars into war industry. Since, in the United States, corporations and the rich are taxed most and taxes are not permitted to rise faster than income, the average John Doe finds himself

*Address to The American Society of Newspaper Editors, as reported in the *New York Times*, 19 May 1966.

better off during war. Thus the government, primarily through war and the graduated income tax, has produced such domestic euphoria that its public expenditures – primarily its expeditures for war and space – have the psychological effect of egoistic ones. Since it is fear – fear of communism – that makes Americans willing to pay the taxes for armaments in the first place, but since these taxes come back to them in good living, we can say that, literally, Americans grow fat on fear. What fear they might have of war is narcotized by good times. When we consider that, in view of Vietnam, the Russians have had to slow down expansion in the production of consumer goods in order to put more effort into the production of armaments, we see that one traditional psychological obstacle to war does not exist for Americans.

CONFUSION BETWEEN FRIEND AND ENEMY. During World War II Japan was our enemy, now she is our friend; the Soviet Union was our friend, now she is our enemy; Germany was our enemy, now part of her is friend, part enemy; France was our friend, now she is almost our enemy; Yugoslavia was our friend, now she is our friend one day, our enemy the next, as our foreign policy shifts. During World War II China was our friend, now she is our enemy. Before the war in the Middle East we were able to live comfortably with our anti-semitism, now we see our government incomprehensibly on Israel's side; during World War II Italy was our enemy, now she is our friend – and so it goes. In the ordinary citizen the result of these wild fluctuations in the definition of enemy and friend can only be mental withdrawal, cynicism and a readiness to resign decisions to 'higher powers' and 'experts'. On the other hand such passivity in the presence of radical alterations in the definition of the enemy could take place only if we had handed over decisions to higher powers in the first place. The American's lack of involvement in anything but his standard of living and his family, plus a persisting feeling of vulnerability, make him accept easily any alteration in foreign policy. Meanwhile, I doubt that, in this, Americans are much different from the rest of the world called civilized.

In this connexion, we see the importance of short-run perceptions. It is as if modern man never committed his perceptual apparatus permanently to any definition. It is disquietingly like the perception of style. Style depends on short-run perceptions; on the fact, for example, that though a dark tie may seem best with one's suit today, there is always present in the mind the reservation that this is not for ever, but only as long as some power defines it as style. I find something similar in the academic world. There is, for example, no commitment in anthropology or sociology to any point of view. Acceptance of contemporary theorists lasts, at the most, just about as long as they are alive. When they die, no one quotes them any more. Sometimes a theory lasts only a semester. While I do not consider acceptance or rejection of a foreign power homologous with style or with acceptance of a social theory, I do believe that all three rely on a condition of contemporary perception – the withholding of commitment to any view of the world. This superficiality, this fundamental impenetrability of the soul, is due to the evanescent quality of modern life and to the basic depression of modern man.

THE INIMICAL FACTOR IN LIFE. A culture has never been found where there was not a permanent inimical factor that served to terrify and to integrate the people and to suffocate deviant opinion. In tribal life the inimical beings are monsters or spirits and outside enemies, defined by tradition as everlastingly dangerous to mankind or to the tribe or both. One is trained from infancy to accept these inimical ones as eternal and unchanging, and no one says they do not exist or that they are friendly or that their friendship can be won. The threat of the inimical stifles thought but also creates social solidarity.

In the contemporary world, as contrasted with the tribal, the inimical lacks *traditional* definition, and the group in power reserves to itself the right, and the power, to define who the inimical shall be. The definition, then, becomes part of the social system: lessons about the inimical are taught to elementary-school children; the mass media scream its name with appropriate invective; the inimical becomes part of the legal system and it becomes incorporated into the economic framework. It becomes as inexorable as a primitive hallucination, and doubting it carries the same punitive social consequences. In the United States the inimical is communism. Incorporated into elementary-school readers and sociological tracts, frozen into supreme-court decisions and loyalty oaths, and consolidated further through embargoes on goods to communist countries, the communist bogy has the qualities of a tribal delusion. The delusion of the 'communist menace' represents the exploitation of man's primordial tendency to define some part of the universe as inimical, in order to prepare the American people for war.

FREEDOM, ENTERPRISE AND DOCILITY. When we consider the international structure of the American corporate community and the fact that the sun never sets on it, it is clear that 'free world' means the part of it that is free for American investment. It is for that reason that Spain, for example, is considered part of the 'free world'. On the other hand, when we realize that there is no owned American investment in communist countries, we comprehend why the communist world is not 'free'. Yet, when we know that the United States supplies heavy machinery which Italy is using in its Fiat installation in the Soviet Union, we understand, in part, why Russia seems 'freer' to us now than it used to be.

Americans are used to the expression 'free enterprise', yet it is clear from the outline of the structure of the American economy that the expression has no meaning at all. The tightly woven fabric of the American economy leaves little room for 'enterprise', and over the past several decades the type of person heading up large corporations has changed from the individual master builder to the long-time-serving, loyal and cautious executive, who is guided by his board of directors, underwriters, accounting and legal firms and research department. Nowadays corporations rarely fire anybody, even at the lower levels; as long as they are docile and fit the over-all gentlemanly pattern of operations, they are moved around in the firm until they find a niche. Decisions are very much by committee and not by individuals. All of this is well known and has been popularized in a penetrating book by William H. White, Jr, called *The Organization Man*.

Similar processes are at work in labour. The ideal American labour leader nowadays is not one who risks injury or death in a strike, but a careful negotiator, who is backed by a team of lawyers and researchers. The labour movement in the United States nowadays is very different from what management confronted in the 1920s, armed for deadly combat. Organized labour is probably the most contented segment of the American population; it has shifted from being the most revolutionary group to being the most conservative.

Along with these alterations in the structure of American political economy there has developed a vast, sheep-like docility in the population. Grazing on the grasses of affluence, the white American population is one of the most docile on earth. This is ideal psychological preparation for war, for docile people make excellent soldiers.

Let me summarize what I have said up to this point about the psychological factors that prepare for war. I have said that feeling vulnerable we are ever on the defensive. TV shows, for adults or for children, that portray individuals and nations under attack are the commonest programme. Meanwhile, as we are frightened into paying heavy taxes to 'save' ourselves and support our wars, we have a wonderful time, for taxes come back to us in increased income. So Americans grow fat on their fear and fear feels good, or, at least, better than it ever did before. It is hard to be against the war in Vietnam if your pay has gone up because of it. I referred to American docility and the readiness to accept as friend the nation that was a foe yesterday and to accept as enemy today the nation that was a friend yesterday. Since, in the United States, one is never threatened, really, by such erratic definitions, but finds, rather, that one's standard of living rises, why object? It is a law of learning theory that organisms tend to respond positively to reward. In the American experience, having enemies has been rewarding. The fact that some people have lost sons is of little consequence, for the personal detachment, withdrawal and uninvolvement of the American, his inability to feel for another person's bereavement, his concern only with what is close to him and with his standard of living, make him impervious to the sorrow of others. Furthermore, as I pointed out, the depressive core in the soul of the American population makes people turn away from the anguish of others, while brooding only on their own. I spoke, then, of the inimical factor in life, of the fact that in the modern, as contrasted with the tribal, world the inimical is selected by the group in power and of the fact that the perceptual functions of the people are shaped to suit this group's objectives. In modern times perception has rapidly evolved away from tradition-determined perceptions of the world to class-determined ones and perception is manipulated by the mass media. So one acquires and puts off one's enemies and friends, one's ideas, one's opinions, and one's tastes somewhat as one changes style. Finally I pointed out the lack of sense in the words 'freedom' and 'enterprise'. The last point I take up is the psychological consequences of the disappearance from life of any real options, of any real freedom.

NO EXIT. It is clear that freedom exists only where there are real options; where the individual, or a nation, in spite of its history, can make a choice that is not over-determined by the system. While it is unlikely that at any time man's choices were *not* over-determined; while it is unlikely that *Homo sapiens* ever had a local or international system that allowed him to invent new solutions to his old problems, I feel that never before have so many felt that they lived in a room with no exit. This results in apathy and withdrawal from life. Meanwhile the attractiveness of withdrawal is enhanced by the high-rising standard of living and the increased possibilities for good times, which narcotize all feeling, and by the extreme danger of going against the multitude. The knowledge that there are no options, the feeling of entrapment, the feeling that one can do nothing because there are no doors, makes its inevitable contribution to war; for not only does it lead to ready acceptance of war as a solution to difficult problems, but it creates docility also. Man is everywhere chained to a system in which he perceives no new options. Yet there are – for the vast and radical political changes that have occurred in the past two generations prove that man can create new options where there seemed to be none.

Imperialism and Revolution in America | *John Gerasis*

One of the things that have struck me in the first few days of this conference is that it has split in half. There are those who are concerned with political matters and those who are primarily interested in psychological problems. Thus 'liberation' has been defined in two ways: liberation from physical oppression, from an outward enemy; and liberation from the psychological oppression of the environment. Behind this divergence of interests, however, is an underlying assumption which I think all of us have made. That is, that the enemy itself, the structure, the society in which we live and from which we suffer, has to be brought down. A re-structuring of society has to take place.

Let us first go back a bit and find out just how that society became as oppressive as it is and what that oppression means to three groups of individuals: those who are in the Third World and who, therefore, feel the oppression materially, physically, militarily and culturally, and who generally react to it violently; those who are conscious of the oppression but cannot differentiate its outward from its inward consequences, who feel that they must seek a new form of consciousness for themselves and hence react generally though not exclusively non-violently (copping out of society or setting up their own communities outside it); and finally those who live within the enemy, within the structure itself, but who suffer directly from it – namely and especially the non-white minorities in the US – and whose reaction normally is violent.

Whatever our reaction to oppression there seems to me to be little doubt that our consciousness of it, on its present wide scale, has come about as a result of the war in Vietnam. Yet there is a great danger in not realizing that the war in Vietnam is no accident, and that America has not suddenly become imperialistic but has always been imperialistic; that America has not just suddenly become brutal, but has always been brutal; that America has not suddenly become racist, but has always been racist.

America's imperialism became clear to the world, except Americans, in 1823 when President Monroe declared what is now known as the Monroe Doctrine. To the US, to liberal rhetoricians, to liberal historians in general, the Monroe Doctrine is considered to be a generous, brave and basically moral declaration. It says, they claim, 'The Americas have to be free, Europe stay out, let the Americas develop by themselves.' This is not the interpretation the Latin Americans give to it. On the contrary, they see the Monroe Doctrine as the first open declaration by the US of its intention to make Latin America its own. They interpret that declaration as saying 'The rest of Europe stay out because Latin America is ours.' And this became quite clear only a year after it was enunciated, in 1824, when Secretary of State (later President) John Quincy Adams told Simón Bolivar, one of the great liberators of Latin America, to stay out of Cuba and Puerto Rico because the Monroe Doctrine 'must not be interpreted as authorization for the weak to be insolent with the strong'.

Of course, the US could not put the Monroe Doctrine into effect when it was dealing with highly developed, highly imperialistic, highly militarized powers. When England took over the Falkland Islands, for example, the United States did not intervene. England then occupied that part of Guatemala which is now called British Honduras and invaded Guatemala, and the US still did not react. That is because the US was always consistent in its imperialism in the sense that it carried it out only in so far as it was capable of doing so. The difference, therefore, between a century ago and today is simply the difference in the US's military strength. But it was imperialistic right from the beginning. It saw, right from the start, the danger of a Latin American union. Simón Bolivar called a conference in 1826 to create a United States of Latin America. The US not only refused to attend – it had been invited – not only put pressure on various delegates to work against it, but also put economic pressure on the small countries of Latin America to destroy it completely. This is what led Bolivar to make that statement which is so well known: 'The United States appear to be destined by providence to plague America with misery in the name of liberty.'

We all know what happened after that. The US went into Mexico, began to intervene throughout the Caribbean, and so on. And the American people developed an attitude in which they considered themselves to be led by destiny to impose upon the world – first on their immediate world and gradually all over the world – their way of looking at things. This was called the 'manifest destiny'.

Liberals will say, and do say, that this policy has never been consistent. They point out, for example, that during this so-called 'manifest destiny' period in the last century, the US Government tried to enforce its neutrality laws and tried to prosecute those who violated them. The big example that liberals give is that in the mid-1800s the US Government tried to hamper and prosecute American privateers, known as the Filibusters. These were individuals who went throughout Latin America to conquer land, to conquer countries, financed by and for the profit of individual American companies.

The most famous of these Filibusters was William Walker. An Ashville-born doctor, lawyer and journalist (who practised none of these professions), Walker invaded Nicaragua, captured Granada and had himself proclaimed – 'elected' –

President of that country. He then sent a message to President Franklin Pierce asking that Nicaragua be admitted to the Union as a Slave State, even though Nicaragua had long outlawed slavery. Walker was operating for American private corporations bent on exploiting Central America. The trouble was that these companies were rivals of Cornelius Vanderbilt's Accessory Transit Company whose Nicaragua concessions Walker, as 'President', had cancelled. Vanderbilt thereupon threw all his money and power behind other forces and they defeated Walker. He was handed over to the US Navy, brought back to the States and put on trial. He admitted that he had violated the Neutrality laws. The evidence against him was overwhelming. And yet, as had happened once before when he tried to conquer Lower California, he was found Not Guilty. In fact the jury cheered him at the end of his trial.

Was the jury corrupt? Was it imperialist itself? Or was it simply reflecting the teachings, the propaganda, the atmosphere of the US? For that, I think we ought to go back briefly to the beginning.

When the first colonizers of North America had successfully established viable societies in their new land they launched themselves westward. Liberal historians tell us that this great pioneering spirit was truly a magnificent impulse, a golden asset in America's formation. In their expansionism to the west the Americans were ruthless, systematically wiping out the whole indigenous population. But they were successful, and by and large that expansion was completed without sacrificing too many of the basic civil rights of the white settlers. Thus early on America began to take pride in its system.

Later, as American entrepreneurs launched the industrialization of their country, they were equally successful. In the process they exploited the new settlers, the working class and their children, but they built a strong economy. Once again they showed themselves and the world that America was a great country, so great in fact that it could not, should not, stop at its own borders. As these entrepreneurs expanded beyond America's borders, mostly via the sea, and so developed America's naval power, they were again successful and once again proved to themselves and to the world how great America was. It did not matter that Jeffersonian democracy, which liberal historians praise as the moral backbone of America's current power, rested on the Haves and excluded the Have-nots to the point where if one did not own property one could not vote. Nor did it matter that Jacksonian democracy, which liberal historians praise even more, functioned in a ruthless, totalitarian setting in which one sector of the economy attempted and by and large succeeded in crushing the other. The rhetoric was pure, the results formidable, and therefore the system was perfect. That system became known as 'The American Way of Life', a way of life in which the successful were the good and the unsuccessful the bad. America was founded very early on the basic premise that he who is poor deserves to be poor, and he who is rich is entitled to the fruits of his power.

Since America was big enough and rich enough to allow its entrepreneurs to become tycoons, while gradually allowing the white poor to demand a fair share – and to a certain extent to obtain it, in terms of *legal* civil rights and a certain mobility – the rhetoric justifying all the murders and all the exploitations became a theory, and out of this theory grew the conviction that America was the greatest country in the world precisely because it allowed the kind of self-determination that it did. From there it was only a step to the conclusion that any country which was not the same was inferior. And the corollary, of course, was that the country which did not follow America's lead would not be great. Finally, it became clear to all Americans that he who is great is good.

The American Way of Life became the personification of morality.

From America's pride in its way of life followed the right to impose that way of life on non-Americans. Americans became superior, self-righteous and pure. The net result was a new Jesuit society. It too carried a sword and a cross. America's sword was its marines; America's cross was American democracy. Under that cross, as under the cross brandished by the Conquistadores of colonial Spain, the US rationalized its colonialism.

The jury that tried Walker for violating America's Neutrality Laws expressed that imperialism, that rationalization, when it cheered Walker out of court. It was simply reflecting its deep-rooted conviction that Nicaragua would be better off as a Slave State in the Union than as a free country outside it. To that jury, as to the American people today, there can be only one democratic system worthy of the name – the American; there can be only one definition of freedom – American free enterprise. Thus there is no need for the State Department to proclaim its imperialist policy. The Vanderbilts, the Rockefellers, the Guggenheims, the United Fruit Company, the Hanna Mining Corporation, the Anaconda Company, can do what they please. They represent democracy, they are the embodiment of freedom. What's more, they know that when the chips are down the American Marines will be right behind them, if not in front of them.

Within the last century America's colonial expansionism, based on and strengthened by the American Way of Life, has become consistently bolder as the US has become consistently stronger. Beginning in 1860, when it invaded Honduras, armed intervention throughout the Caribbean and Central America became commonplace. Teddy Roosevelt, the dollar diplomacy, the big stick, etc. are all quite well known and there is no need to go into them now.

But one thing inevitably happened, and that is that whenever the US subjugated people, people rebelled. These rebellions had to be quelled by armed strength. But it always had to be the US Marines because there was nobody else around to quell them. In Haiti the rebels were called the Cacos. In Nicaragua the guerillas were led by Augusto Cesar Sandino, who fought the US Marines from 1926 to 1934 without ever being defeated although the Marines razed to the ground various towns in Nicaragua and, by accident, in Honduras to boot. In 1934 Sandino was offered negotiations and he was foolish enough to accept them, to believe the offer. So he went to the American Embassy, and as he walked out of the American Embassy compound, while he was still on American Embassy grounds, he was assassinated.

Such incidents are very common in Latin America, so much so that no intelligent rebel who has popular support can ever again trust negotiation offers by the US unless he can determine the setting and the terms of these negotiations. (It seems that the Vietnamese have read American history very carefully, and that is why the terms of any kind of negotiations which are not set by them are, quite rightly, unacceptable to them.)

On 4 March 1933 the US officially changed its policy, and it is this change that interests me most. Officially the change was known as the end of imperialism. In his Inauguration Address, Franklin Delano Roosevelt told the world that American imperialism was over and that from now on the US would be a good neighbour. He voted in favour of the Non-Intervention Pledge at the 1933 Montevideo Inter-American Conference, promised Latin American countries tariff reductions, exchanged trade agreements and a year later abrogated completely the Platt Amendment. His top diplomat, Sumner Wells, said in 1935: 'It is my belief that American capital invested abroad, in fact as well as in theory, be subordinate to the authority of the people of the country where it is located.' A very radical change!

Really? In fact, only the form of America's intervention had changed. F.D.R. was the most intelligent imperialist the US has had. As a liberal, he knew the value of rhetoric. As a capitalist, he knew that he who dominates the economy dominates the politics. As long as American interventionism for economic gain had to be defended by US Marines, rebellions and revolutions would be inevitable. One can always see a Marine: He is an enemy who is present and there is no way of hiding him, of making believe that he is there as a friend. The Marine is always identifiable for what he is.

But Roosevelt understood that if there were no Marines, if instead the oppressors were the local militia, police or military forces (whose loyalty to American commercial interests could be guaranteed by their economic ties to those interests), then it would be difficult, perhaps impossible, for local patriots to finger the enemy. Thus Roosevelt launched a brilliant series of policies designed to tie Latin American countries to the US.

In 1938 F.D.R. set up the Interdepartmental Committee of Co-operation with American Republics, which was in effect the precursor of today's Technical Aid Programme of the Organization of American States. The O.A.S. itself grew out of the Pan-American Union, which had been set up by the Secretary of State as 'an ideal economic complement to the United States.' F.D.R.'s Interdepartmental Committee assured Latin America's dependency on the US for technical progress. During the War the Department of Agriculture sent to Latin America soil-conservation research teams which helped increase Latin America's dependency on one-crop economies. In 1940 F.D.R. said that the US Government and US private businesses should invest heavily in Latin America, in order 'to develop sources of raw materials needed in the United States'. On 26 September 1940 he increased the limitation of the Export/Import Bank, which is an arm of the American Treasury, from $100 million to $700 million; and by the time of Pearl Harbor most Latin American countries had received development loans from which they have yet to disengage themselves.

Today Latin Americans use up to 40 per cent of their foreign earnings just to pay off the interest, or the service charge, on loans from the industrialized world – not the capital, not the principal, just the interest and the service charge.

Roosevelt's policies were so successful that his successors, liberals all whether Republican or Democrat, continued and strengthened them. By 1950, after a decade and a half of *talking* democracy, the US controlled 70 per cent of Latin America's sources of raw materials, and 50 per cent of its gross national product. Latin American reformers thought, precisely because they saw the outward signs, the outward facets of political democracy, that they could use it to gain power and change the structure. But of course in an underdeveloped country, where illiterates can't vote, 70 per cent of the population are eliminated. And even if an illiterate can vote, as he can for example in Chile, he must have an address, so that if he lives in a slum he is eliminated anyway; 30 per cent of Chile's population live in slums.

Besides, as F.D.R. and the American liberals who were making foreign policy understood very well, if one has political freedom but not economic freedom one cannot wage campaigns. One has to have newspapers, one has to have radios. Who controls the money? Trade unions? Even today only 1 per cent of unions in the underdeveloped world have check-off clauses because that little percentage, those few pennies that would automatically come out of the worker's salary into the funds of the union, make the difference between getting a glass of milk for a child or not. So the unions themselves don't insist, don't try to impose check-off clauses. There is no slush fund, there is no surplus with which the disenfranchised can wage a political campaign. They can't get the press, they can't get the radios, and they can't even afford to pay people full-time to run a campaign against the established order.

The US understood this very well and so it insisted upon political democracy without economic democracy. The US even tried to bring down a few dictators here and there, just to show that it was genuinely interested in democratic process. This was especially true under Kennedy's Alliance for Progress (though it had a boomerang effect in that more dictators are in power today than before the Alliance for Progress was started). If the US could demonstrate to the world that under its aegis Latin America was moving towards a democratic process, with free elections, then the accusation that it is an oppressor would not hold. And this argument was effective even with Latin Americans, who ought to have known better.

Occasionally, through flukes – because a politician presented himself as a mild nationalist and then turned out to be a socialist, or something like that – the Latin American people got a few honest men elected. One was Juan José Arevalo in Guatemala; another was Jacobo Arbenz after him. Between the two of them they changed the general aspect of their country. They legalized the rights of labour, they gave the unions the right to negotiate directly with the plantation owners (United Fruit in this particular case), they allowed the press to be free, etc., all things which had never occurred before. But they didn't really do anything to the economy. And just before the Agrarian Reform Law of 1952 the statistics, according to the United Nations, showed that if one counted each foreign corporation as one individual, 98 per cent of Guatemala's cultivated land was owned by exactly 142 people in a population of 3,500,000. Only 10 per cent of the population attended school at that time.

Arevalo and Arbenz did try to change these conditions. In 1952 they proclaimed Decree 900, a land reform which called for the expropriation and redistribution of *uncultivated* land above a basic acreage. Decree 900 specifically exempted all intensively cultivated land, which amounted to only 5 per cent of the over-one-thousand-hectare farms, and ordered that all absentee-owned property be redistributed. Compensation was offered in 20-year bonds at 3 per cent interest, assessed according to declared tax value. American liberal economists and agronomists applauded Decree 900. On page 179 of *Latin American Issues*, which was published by the semi-official Twentieth Century Fund, one may read: 'For all the fury it produced, Decree 900, which had its roots in the Constitution of 1945, is a remarkably mild and fairly sound piece of legislation.'

But United Fruit owned most of the land, and United Fruit obviously didn't want to be expropriated. When Arbenz actually took away the land – the unexploited, uncultivated land – and distributed it to 180,000 peasants, the US immediately condemned it as communist, and convened the O.A.S. in Caracas to make that condemnation official. It then found a right-wing Colonel, Castillo Armas, a graduate of US Command School at Fort Leavenworth, fed him arms, trained him, gave him planes, even piloted some of the planes and finally through him brought down Arbenz.

Since then the US has intervened again repeatedly in Latin America, most visibly in the Dominican Republic. As a result of that intervention, in which 43,000 American troops were used to put down a nationalist rebellion of 4,000 armed men, the US has made it clear that it will never allow any Latin American government to break America's rigid economic control.

That control today extends to 85 per cent of the sources

of raw material. One American company, United Fruit, controls over 50 per cent of the foreign earnings, and thus of the whole economic structure, of six Latin American countries. In Venezuela the Standard Oil Company of New Jersey (Rockefeller), through its subsidiary, the Creole Oil Corporation, controls all the bases of the industrializing process. Venezuela is potentially the second richest country in the world. Its $500 million plus net annual revenue from oil could alone guarantee every family, counting 6½ persons per family, an annual income of $500 plus. But in fact 40 per cent of the population lives outside the money economy, 22 per cent are unemployed and the country must use $100 million a year to import foodstuffs (from the US), while there is enough land under proper cultivation to produce a surplus of food for export. By and large such conditions prevail in all Latin American countries.

The continent as a whole uses, as I said, 40 per cent of its foreign earnings to pay off interest. The Alliance for Progress claims that it is helping Latin America to industrialize on a social-progress basis. Now more than six years old, it has chalked up remarkable successes, namely: right-wing coups in Bolivia, Argentina, Brazil, Honduras, Guatemala, Ecuador, the Dominican Republic and Salvador. In exchange, US businessmen have remitted to the US $5 billion worth of profits, while investing, on paper, $2 billion. The Alliance itself, which is supposed to lend money for strictly social progress projects, has kept 86 per cent of its outlay for credits for American goods – credits which are guaranteed, must be guaranteed, by Latin American governments and repaid in dollars.

Under President Johnson there are no longer any illusions. Johnson is on record as having said, at Camp Stanley, Korea, in 1966: 'Don't forget there are two hundred million of us in a world of three billion. They want what we've got, and we're not going to give it to them.'

Karl Marx once warned that the first revolutionary wave in an imperialized country will come about as the result of frustration by the national bourgeoisie, which will have reached a stage of development where it will have accumulated enough capital to want to become competitive with the imperializing corporations. American businessmen knew that Karl Marx was right and they have made sure that this does not happen. As American corporations became acutely plagued by surplus goods, they realized that they must expand their markets in underdeveloped countries. To do so, however, they would have to help develop a national bourgeoisie which could purchase these goods. This national bourgeoisie, like all such classes in colonized countries, had to be created through service industries, yet it had somehow to be limited so that it did not become economically independent.

The solution was simple. The American corporations, having set up, say, an assembly plant in Sao Paulo or Buenos Aires which they called Brazilian or Argentinian, decided actually to help create the subsidiary corporations with local money. Take General Motors, for example. First it brought down its cars in various pieces, called 'parts', thus eliminating import duties. Then it assembled them in Sao Paolo and called them Brazil-made. Next it shopped around for local entrepreneurs to launch the subsidiary industries – seat covers, spark plugs, etc. Normally the landed oligarchy and entrepreneurs in the area would do their own investing in these subsidiary industries and, having successfully amassed large amounts of capital, would bind together to create their own car industry competitive with General Motors. It was this that had to be avoided. General Motors first offered local entrepreneurs contracts by which it helped finance the servicing industries. Then it brought the entrepreneurs' capital together into huge holding corporations, which in turn it rigidly controlled. The holding corporations became very successful, making the entrepreneurs happy; and everyone forgot about the local competitive car industry, making General Motors happy.

This procedure is best employed by IBEC, Rockefeller's mammoth investing corporation in Latin America. IBEC claims to be locally owned by Latin Americans since the Rockefellers do not hold a controlling interest. And this is true. Depending on the country – Peru, Venezuela, Colombia – only from 25 to 45 per cent of the shares are US owned. But when one corporation owns 45 per cent while thousands of individual investors split the other 55 per cent, the corporation sets policy, in the US as well as abroad. Besides, IBEC is so successful that local entrepreneurs think American even before IBEC does. In any case, the result of these holding corporations is that the national bourgeoisie in Latin America has been eliminated. It is an American bourgeoisie. IBEC and the other holding corporations use this combined local/US capital to invest in all sorts of profitable ventures, from supermarkets to assembly plants. Naturally these new corporations are set up where they can bring the most return. IBEC is not going to build a supermarket in the Venezuelan province of Falcón, where there are guerrillas right now and where the population lives outside the money economy and hence could not buy at the supermarket anyway; moreover there are no roads to take the goods to the supermarket, if one were to be built in Falcón.

This is why, at the 1967 Punta del Este Conference, it was the US that pushed for the Common Market. And this is why the American public has been so fooled by the editorials in the *New York Times* and in the *Washington Post* and everywhere else, which made it seem that suddenly the US, even under Johnson, was taking a liberal attitude since it was fostering a Common Market in Latin America.

What is actually happening becomes plainer if one

considers the implications of this Common Market for, for example, General Motors. General Motors builds cars in Sao Paulo, and it has a certain gradually increasing Americanized bourgeoisie in Brazil that keeps buying these cars. But that's not enough. General Motors would like to expand. How could it expand in the rest of Latin America? One way would be by building another assembly plant, say in Lima. But that is very costly, involving actual investment. As there is already an assembly plant in Sao Paulo, wouldn't it be better to send the cars across to Peru already made? But there are import duties of up to 150 per cent on finished products. So what happens? Break down the barriers, create a Common Market. Anything 'built' in Brazil would then be able to enter Peru tax free. And these 'Brazilian-made' cars are being made in Brazil, therefore they can go into Peru tax free. Thus General Motors will soon be sending its cars, which cost them $1,000 to make and which are being sold right now at $12,000 for an ordinary Chevrolet, into various Latin American countries knowing that other foreign manufacturers will not be able to compete because their cars would have to come by sea, from outside the Common Market area, and hence would have to pay 150 per cent import duties.

Having so tied up the local economies, the US rarely needs to intervene with Marines to guarantee friendly governments. The local military, bought by American national interest, guarantees friendly regimes with the approval of the local press, the local legal political parties, the local cultural centres, all of which are controlled by the local money, which is American.

Latin American reformers have finally realized all this. They know now that the only way to break the structure is to break it, which means a violent revolution. Hence there are no reformers in Latin America today. There are either those, whatever they call themselves, who really will do

America's bidding, or there are revolutionaries. For Latin America – and I would conjecture that this is true for all the underdeveloped world – there is only one solution, and that solution is a violent revolution.

But we in the US, or here in England, are not part of the underdeveloped world. So why should we be ready to sacrifice our lives fighting for Latin America? After all, we do not suffer from these conditions, the structure just described is not ours. But then what is our structure, for us who live within the developed world? Well, for one thing it has fooled most of us with its claim that we enjoy economic freedom. This participatory capitalism, which is roughly now around 20 per cent – that is, roughly one fifth of the American public actually owns one share or more of an American capitalist enterprise – gives us a feeling that we have a direct say, even a direct share in our future. Theoretically every stock-owner could attend an American corporation board meeting and vote on its policies. One reads about such events all the time, especially in the *Daily News*, which loves to photograph that little woman who shows up with one share and demands the floor in a meeting of I.T. & T. or some other huge corporation and gets it, takes the microphone and insults all the managerial staff which is up front. This gives those living under capitalism a feeling of participation in the economic structure, and fortifies the myth that we live by the law. And the liberals, who are afraid of violence because it will be directed at them – since they are direct participants in, if not the creators of, the system – insist that such rule of law is what is most to be defended.

I went to North Vietnam as an investigator for the Bertrand Russell Peace Foundation as a preparation for the International War Crimes Tribunal. Before I went I talked to many of my friends in New York and tried to gain their support for such a Tribunal. I talked specifically to one 'revolutionary' who has written a book defending revolution in Latin America. This 'revolutionary', in reality just a liberal, refused to support the Tribunal because, he said: 'It is immoral and will defeat everything it is directed at, everything which we really fight for – justice under law.' This meant to him that if the Tribunal was successful it would be throwing out into the world, without a law to justify it, the verdict on the perpetrators of the war crimes. In other words, the direct logical consequence of the International War Crimes Tribunal is to say to all of us, to any one of us, that if Johnson is guilty we are all morally justified in executing him.

I said, 'Yes, if he is found guilty that would be the logical consequence of the verdict at the International War Crimes Tribunal.' And his answer was: 'As much as I personally would like to see Johnson dead, what you're doing is putting morality above the law, and this will destroy any political system.' That is the liberal position: respect for Law. The law doesn't have to be moral because it defends that which already exists. The liberal's myth is that through the rule of law justice ultimately triumphs. And although he can be shown that it is under the rule of law that we butcher people in Santo Domingo, that it is under the rule of law that we go into Vietnam to wipe out a population with napalm, nevertheless the liberal will insist that it must be under the rule of law that we must put an end to all these crimes.

This myth is now part and parcel of the American Way of Life which I described earlier. This Way of Life is the key to the paradox that America is the most imperialistic country in the world, yet Americans claim that they have never been imperialistic at all. A system of law has always been essential to the American Way of Life. This system justifies repressions, rationalizes oppressions, codifies frustrations. But to the world we exploit, and to ourselves as we feel futile and one-dimensional, as Marcuse would say, that system of law serves to eliminate choices. Thus we react by focusing on our inner selves.

We go to a university and we are taught platitudes. We graduate from universities and we have only one of two choices: either to retreat, to cop out, or else to join into the system which will make us into one of those cards that Jules Henry so well described yesterday.

But this stifling, frustrating world we live in is possible only because most of us never have to worry about the basic necessities of life. In the world we exploit, however, it does not and cannot work the same way. In Latin America people die of old age at twenty-eight, the vast majority of the population does not eat more than 500 calories a day, illiteracy is higher now than ten years ago, and fewer people have potable water today than yesterday. That kind of poverty is an abstraction for us whites. No matter how much we see it around us we really can't understand what poverty is because we do not suffer it; at least not like an Indian peasant I once met in Bolivia. This peasant woman had four bowls of rice and five children. She gave her four eldest children a bowl, but not the youngest one sitting in the corner. I asked her, 'Why aren't you feeding that child?' She said, 'He's the weakest, he's the youngest, he's going to be the first to die anyway. I don't have enough food for all five so I have to make a choice, and I'm not going to feed the one that's going to die first.'

When you are forced into this kind of choice, you hate – the hate that Che Guevara talks about, the hate that leads you to kill. Che says 'Our soldiers must hate. A people without hatred cannot vanquish a brutal enemy.' And this is certainly true – but not for us white Anglo-Saxons. We don't have that kind of hatred. Our hatred is intellectual, not the hatred that comes from having to choose not to feed one out of five children. We are not faced with this kind of hatred. We do reject this society and its values, and we know that it leads to such real hatred. Yet all we seem capable of doing is pulling out. And so we pull out and we become diggers, hippies, drug addicts, whatever else there is.

What does this lead to? Well, it is disruptive and therefore it is to be encouraged. If you keep pulling out from society you are obviously pushing the contradictions that exist within that society and making them wider. But is it effective? I have nothing against hippies, I have nothing against diggers. On the contrary, I consider them my allies. They are in opposition to the society which tries to subjugate them. But can they be successful?

Suppose the Provos or the hippies or the diggers or what have you continue to have influence, continue to spread from what they are now – which is, let's face it, a minute minority, so small that, at least in the US, it can be incorporated into the system without difficulty and without threat to the society. Suppose it widens, though. What is the Establishment going to do? Will it tolerate it? If the Establishment is fighting in Vietnam to propagate its society, its Way of Life, its structure, what makes you think that it is not going to fight against the diggers or the hippies or anybody else that can threaten it? That diggers are not being thrown into jail, or are not being lynched, is because they are not a threat. That I'm not in jail is because I'm no threat. That we can all come here, and go back, and perhaps at the worst, if we go to Cuba or Vietnam, lose our passports for a month, is because we are harmless. Even when we get fired from one university, we get re-hired by another. But should we become threatening, then we'll be hit. If the US can smash people all over the world with guns and napalm, it certainly is not going to be gentle about the way it tries to suppress hippies. This is not speculation. Look at the way the US is hitting the blacks. It tried to keep them down by the rule of law without organized established violence. That failed, so now it uses the rule of law to justify its violence.

The blacks are being hit constantly. But they are reacting. And they are doing so the only way they know how: a tooth for a tooth, an eye for an eye. But it is an eye *after* an eye, a tooth *after* a tooth. In other words, it is a reaction to the violence of the administration. And that is why it is still losing. When you have a confrontation on the spur of the moment, when you have a reaction against a white cop who kills a Negro boy, then you have a slaughter, then you have twenty-eight Negroes dead. Such statistics, if they keep going, aren't going to help very much in the long run.

What must the blacks do then? They must realize that they are like the people of the underdeveloped world. They must learn from them too. When you are in a minority, when you are more or less unarmed, when all the others have the loudspeakers as well as the guns, there is only one way to defeat them – that is to fight them on your terms. Che Guevera made this quite clear and with success. The Black Liberation Movement in the US must do the same thing. When it attacks the white oppressive forces, it must be the one to decide when and how.

But even so, the black population accounts for only 10 per cent of the US, and it lives in very clearly marked and dif-ferentiable areas – the ghettoes. When the US, when the Establishment gets put against the wall by the guerrilla movement in Latin America, it will most likely resort to atomic weapons – at least tactical. Che knew this and tried to prepare for it. When the American ghettoes get to the point where they can provide a genuine revolutionary force, then the white suppressive forces will hit them, not with billy clubs but with machine guns. And the Negroes must be ready for that time too.

The only way that they can do this is by an organization that is nation-wide. Alone, the Negroes are isolatable. A whole ghetto can be wiped out. Alone, American revolu-tionaries can be picked up, sent to concentration camps, executed. The only possibility is to fight on all fronts. This is the same lesson that Che Guevara learned from the failures of guerrilla movements throughout Latin America from 1961 through 1965. In the Peruvian hills of the Andes in 1965 the MIR, a very valiant and noble guerrilla group with mass peasant support, gained sufficient strength to go into phase 2 of the guerrilla war – open confrontation with the enemy. It was then hit by napalm bombs. The guerrillas didn't expect that, they had underestimated the enemy, underestimated his cruelty. They got hit by napalm and most of their leaders were killed. This will happen to any of us who seriously threaten the corporation-elite which dominates American economy, dominates its aspect of so-called political democracy, and dominates most of the underdeveloped world and tries to dominate the rest of it. Yesterday in a seminar here, everybody was asking, 'How do you fight this corporation-elite, how do you destroy this structure?' And no one had any sure overall answer. Yet there were all sorts of detail-type answers. For one thing, as somebody mentioned, when the blacks revolt in the ghetto of a city, whites in the rest of the city could go around pulling – if they are incapable of sniping at the cops – down all the fire alarms. One can blow up trains, blow up factories, one can infiltrate a draft board and burn its records. One can launch picket lines against banks and industries instead of government agencies. One can organize a massive sit-in in I.T.&T. or the power companies. But what good would all these courageous acts achieve unless there is an organizational structure behind them, a programme?

Revolutions are never created by terrorists. Terrorism can and often does help revolution, but only in conjunction with something else, only when accompanied by a revolutionary programme. And where is the revolutionary programme of the US? Where is that programme that says that we must nationalize General Motors, and explains what we will do with General Motors; that we must nationalize I.T.&T. and what we will do with I.T.&T.?

Such a programme comes out of an organization, an organization that functions not just to give orders – 'You, go there and shoot this man! You, go there and disrupt this!' – but an organization that is revolutionary by virtue of the fact that it groups all of those who are genuinely opposed to the structure into a disciplined, dedicated body willing jointly and individually to give up the 'good life'.

I quite understand the New Left's repugnance to 'organization' when it means Stalinism. Indeed I share that repugnance. But there is no law that says that a national revolutionary party must be Stalinist. That it must mirror the parties existing in Soviet Russia, or in China or anywhere else. Cubans didn't think so, for example. The Cubans have developed their own Marxism. They have made mistakes, but gradually they have evolved their own theory, in their own context, for their own country. And they found that the one way to guarantee that their people are genuinely free is not elections, is not free press, is not all the trappings of the so-called political democracy that we have, but simply to arm their people. They have discovered that when the people are armed, one can be fairly sure that the government can rule not only by the consent but also, and more importantly, by the active participation of the people.

Well, there is no law that says we can't develop our own form of communism, or socialism, or X-ism. But it must be done through an organization, for without this we remain isolated and thus ineffective. Or else we are eliminated – either by being bought or by being physically silenced.

The peoples of the underdeveloped world will rebel because they are hungry, because they are exploited, because they are dominated by foreigners. The American blacks will rebel because they are not allowed to live like whites unless they forgo dignity. In both cases their rebellions, generated by necessity, lead and have already led to militant organizations which can make the most of the lack of resources available.

The whites, however, are lost. They do not starve, they do not suffer. The dignity they lack is interpreted as personal – the one-dimensionality of their souls. I am pointing out here that the cause of their mental torment is fundamentally the same: the brutal but intelligent, totalitarian but liberal, constraining but law-respecting capitalist structure which thrives off the physical anguish of the rest of the world. Thus, we white, Anglo-Saxon, alienated, self-conscious, middle-class tools of the structure must rebel too. To be effective we need a programme. To have a programme we need a national organization. To be willing to accept such an organization – and to safeguard it against Stalinism – we must be aware of why we oppose the structure. We do so not for material gain. Thus we do so on moral grounds.

So, after our quick historical survey, we return to our first discussion and find that for those who suffer from lack of necessities, liberation is to fight; while for those who have the necessities and more, liberation is to break the restrictions and establish a new society that will allow all men to talk about their souls. But that new society cannot exist unless it fights and destroys individual greed. Therefore we who wish to liberate our souls must first establish Socialist Man, and in order to do that we must first join our suffering brothers in their struggle. We must become revolutionaries, too.

The Future of Capitalism | *Paul Sweezy*

When I proposed the subject 'The Future of Capitalism', I had in mind not specific predictions about what is going to happen to capitalism, but rather a way of looking at the problem, the appropriate and fruitful method of analysing the future of capitalism. It is no mystery, no secret from anybody who has been at all familiar with what I have written that I think capitalism has a dim future. But that in itself is of course nothing new; it is what not only Marxists but many other radicals have been saying for well over a hundred years. Capitalism has nevertheless outlasted many expectations and probably will still outlast many expectations; and the analytical problem of diagnosing its future remains, I believe, as important as it ever was.

What I would like to do is to sketch for you three major approaches to the problem and indicate why I think the more traditional and common approaches are wrong, and lead to no useful results; why the approach that I've numbered three is the appropriate one for dealing with this problem.

The first approach, which is characteristic of bourgeois economics and unfortunately also of a certain kind of Marxism – that which is primarily focused on so-called breakdown problems – puts most of its attention on the dynamics of capitalism in the advanced countries of Western Europe and North America. It tends to ask such questions as: have the business cycle and other forms of economic fluctuations been brought under some reasonable control? What about the problem of technology, of automation, of capitalism's ability to absorb technical change? What about the problems of international trade and international monetary flexibility? What about the problems of corporate structure? And so on. Are all of these problems manageable within the framework of the basic private enterprise, market-orientated, profit-motivated economic order? And I think if you spend some time in an academic community in this country or the US, you'll find that these are the central issues which are discussed whenever this subject of the future of capitalism comes up.

This is a completely inadequate framework within which to analyse the future of capitalism. The trouble is, very simply put, that capitalism in the advanced countries, in its traditional homelands where it had its birth and from which it has spread, does not exist in isolation, does not exist in a passive or unreactive environment. On the contrary, it exists as what is in many respects a minority part of the total world society and economy; and its functioning is decisively influenced by the interaction between what happens in the advanced capitalist countries and in the environment. The environment in certain dimensions is considerably larger than the advanced capitalist world itself. In population and production terms, put very roughly, we can say that the advanced capitalist countries comprise around 20 per cent of the world's population and produce about 60 per cent of the world's output; whereas the centrally planned, non-capitalist communist if you like, countries account for around 30 per cent of the population and also about 30 per cent of the world's output. And that leaves what is commonly referred to nowadays as the Third World with something like 50 per cent of the world's population and only 10 per cent of the world's output.

I use the term 'Third World' not only because it has become accepted terminology but also because it is brief and convenient. But I want to stress and demonstrate that it really is not an appropriate term. The Third World is not really third at all – it is a part of one of the other two worlds, and that I think is crucial to an understanding of the whole problem of the future of capitalism.

Approach number two takes account of the fact that the advanced capitalist countries do not exist in isolation, but rather in a quantitively large and qualitatively active environment. This is recognized by an electric sort of bourgeois economics which has flourished since the Second World War, often called 'The Economics of Development' and it seems to be almost equally characteristic of the economic theory of the Soviet Union and the countries in the communist world which are ideologically oriented towards the Soviet Union. This approach either states or implies that there was a time, long ago, when the whole world was underdeveloped, and some time around four centuries ago, an area in Western Europe 'took off' and started to develop in a capitalist way. Why it did this is a controversial subject, on which there is no general agreement, but perhaps this is not a very crucial problem from the point of view of the present-day diagnosis. The developing countries' take-off – you will no doubt recognize the terminology of Walt Rostow, one of the leading ideologists of the American liberal establishment today – enabled these areas to shoot ahead, develop for a number of centuries, leaving the rest of the world behind in their original state of underdevelopment. Then, as a result of the two world wars and various historical accidents, a part of the underdeveloped world broke away and, in a different institutional and structural context, generated its own take-off; that is to say, under the aegis of central planning, state-ownership and general economic regimentation. So that now there was a three-part world, not a two-part world, the one that had taken off several centuries ago, comprising the advanced capitalist countries; the one that had taken off under centrally planned systems very recently; and still that 50 per cent of the world's population which remained at the starting post in a state of underdevelopment, this then being dubbed the Third World.

In these circumstances, the Third World, having seen the possibilities of development, technological change, accumulation of capital and technology, rising living standards, and so on, becomes infected with a desire to take off and enjoy these fruits itself. And here are those two paths that can be followed: which is the Third World going to take? The other side of this coin is that the two systems, the advanced capitalist and the communist, each sees its own future as determined by whether it can attract into its orbit, into its wake, this vast remaining area of the world, comprising upwards of half of its population. That system which succeeds in attracting into its orbit the Third World will ultimately be the victor in what is then called the Great Contest. And I think you can see here that this is the fundamental ideology of the whole liberal establishment in the US and its acolytes elsewhere, where everything depends upon somehow getting the Third World on our side, developing it, and teaching it how to follow in our footsteps. It is also the basic ideology of Soviet peaceful co-existence and peaceful competition. These are merely two different ways of looking at what is essentially the same ideological conception.

I would like to suggest that this second approach, while superior to the first in that it does not ignore the environment in which the advanced capitalist countries exist, is nevertheless completely and utterly misleading and without diagnostic value. And the basic reason – and I think if one grasps this, one has the key to all of modern history – is that it is absurd to picture the whole world of, say, 1500 or any prior date, as being in the state of underdevelopment in which the Third World exists today. *Un*developed if you like by present-day scientific standards; *under*developed in the sense that Africa and Latin America and most of Asia are underdeveloped today, not at all. In fact every one of the continents had, at one time or another, produced a very high level of civilization, with the possible exception of North America. And the heights reached materially and culturally and ideologically in various parts of what are now the underdeveloped world were, of course, extraordinarily impressive by the standards of the day, and in many respects by standards of our time as well.

What happened was something quite different from this mechanical picture of everybody sitting there in a state of underdevelopment and suddenly one small area springing out ahead and outdistancing the rest. What happened was a far from idyllic picture. Capitalism in its homelands advanced from the very beginning by subjugating, plundering, exploiting, and re-shaping the environment in which it existed. The result was to transfer wealth from the periphery to the metropolis, and correspondingly to destroy the old society in the periphery and re-organize it on a dependent satellite basis. This is one aspect of the process. The other was that the wealth plundered, sucked out of the environment, out of the periphery, became the basis for the rapid development of the metropolis. This was the real economic and social basis of the take-off, and without the wealth plundered from the periphery it is extraordinarily doubtful if there would have been this phenomenon of the take-off at all.

Of course, this process has been repeated again and again for many centuries, and always on a larger and larger scale. It really dates from a good deal earlier than the 15th and 16th centuries. I tend to agree with the analysis of Oliver Cox's book *The Foundation of Capitalism,* in which he regards Venice, beginning in the 7th and 8th centuries, as the first genuine capitalist state, which expanded into the hinterland, subdued, plundered, transferred wealth, and developed a highly finished bourgeois culture. Subsequently the same process happened in many other Italian city states, in the Hanseatic cities of Northern Europe; and finally with the opening up of the overseas territories – I am you will notice careful to avoid saying 'the discovery of the new world' – the process shifted, or the centre of gravity shifted, first to Spain and Portugal, and then to Holland, France and England, under whose aegis the new commercial capitalism was inserted into every corner of the world. This, however, was by no means the end of the matter. As the 19th century rolled on, other capitalist centres, particularly the US and Germany and Japan, got into the act, and, by the end of the 19th century the whole world had been thoroughly polarized between a relatively small advanced capitalist metropolis concentrated in a few countries mostly in western Europe and northern America, i.e. the vast underdeveloped and underdeveloping periphery on which it rested and from which it drew a large part of its sustenance.

Now look at what happened to the subjugated and exploited countries and regions. In every case where the pre-existing social order was incompatible with, or stood in the way of the exploitative activities of the conquerors – and in every case the existing society did stand in their way and did inhibit their activities – that order was forcibly transformed and destroyed, with in every case dire consequences for the local cultures and population.

In their frantic hunt for gold, the Portuguese and Spaniards not only seized all they could lay their hands on, but forced the natives into the mines where they perished in droves. The native populations of the Caribbean area were quite literally wiped out within two or three generations, and in much of Central and South America the Indians could survive at all only by retreating into the forests or the mountains. To provide needed labour for the mines and plantations the exploiters developed the slave trade. Large parts of Africa were turned into hunting-grounds for slaves, and of course the society from which the slaves were extracted, and those to which they were sent, were totally transformed. In the Caribbean, Central and South America, and Africa – in that area which is connected by the southern Atlantic – we can see in what may be its purest form the other side of this coin in the amassing of huge fortunes by the slave traders of Liverpool and other English port cities as well as those of France and New England. The generation of underdevelopment took a somewhat different but no less spectacular course in the Far East. The Dutch plundered the Indies and then organized one of the most efficient programmes of continuing exploitation in the colonial world. The British in India are probably the most famous case of all: what had been, not long before the British appeared on the scene, one of the most advanced civilizations in the world, was mercilessly robbed and turned into one of the poorest and most backward countries in the world.

And the other side of the coin, as always, was the accumulation of wealth in the metropolis. Eric Williams, now Prime Minister of Trinidad and Tobago, said in his very useful and revealing monograph *Capitalism and Slavery* that the industrial revolution in England was financed from the profits, direct and indirect, of Negro slavery in the West Indies. Brooks Adams in his book *The Law of Civilization in Decay* gave the credit to the loot from India. Both of them were right.

And then after the conquerors, the first generations of subjugation, came the investors, the traders, the bankers, the administrators and advisors – all those who made it their business to turn the colonies and semi-colonies into lasting sources of profit for the metropolis. As a result of their efforts a characteristic pattern of economic relations developed between the centre and the periphery. The periphery came to specialize in producing raw materials needed in the centre and providing a market for the latter's manufactured goods. At the same time, most of the businesses in the periphery fell into the hands of the capitalists of the centre, and the 'lion's share' of the profits flowed into their pockets.

The underdevelopment of the periphery was thus frozen and perpetuated, while the centre was enabled to continue to develop with the aid of the wealth drained out of its satellites.

At this point, I would like to digress and point out that this pattern of a developed and wealthy centre and an impoverished periphery by no means applies only to the relations between the advanced capitalist countries and the colonial and semi-colonial countries. This, to be sure, is its largest and most spectacular application. But within both parts it also applies. So, for example, you have a country like Brazil, in terms of natural resources and geographical possibilities one of the wealthiest countries in the world. There you have a concentration of wealth and industry in a very small triangle around Rio de Janeiro, Belo Horizonte, and Sao Paulo, while the rest of the country continues to underdevelop in dreadful poverty. You have the same thing within the advanced capitalist metropolises themselves: after all Harlem and Park Avenue are only two or three miles apart, a case of extreme wealth and extreme poverty sitting by each other cheek by jowl. Or look out from the rooftops of Copacabana in Rio at the lovely hillsides, and then look a little more carefully and you will see the famous *favelas*, i.e., some of the worst slums in the world on those hillsides.

Development on the one side and underdevelopment on the other are in mutual and dialectical interdependence. This is the whole history of capitalism from the beginning. It repeats itself on every conceivable scale. These are the two sides of the capitalist coin, absolutely as indivisible as Siamese twins. And until you learn this, until you make it a part of your everyday thinking you will be misled again and again and again by the propaganda which comes at you all the time, which attempts to separate things which belong together, to make out that development is the good side while underdevelopment is the accidental bad side, to pretend that we can have the one without the other. It's not true. It's not true, and until that is understood there can be no really constructive analytical thinking about the problem of the future of the capitalist system.

Against this background one can easily see how false and misleading it is to divide the world into the part which took off into development, and that which remained behind in underdevelopment. Historically speaking, the development of the developed part is the result and counterpart of the underdevelopment of the underdeveloped part. Capitalist development – I repeat myself because, if you get anything out of my talk, this is what I want you to get and take away with you – capitalist development inevitably produces development at one pole and underdevelopment at the other. The advanced capitalist countries and the underdeveloped countries are not two separate worlds; they are the top and bottom sides of one and the same world. So the whole notion of a Third World is really misleading and should be abandoned – not that I think it is likely to be because it is too deeply engrained into the terminology now. But we have continuously to keep in mind that it is a convenient *façon de parler* and not at all a description of a socio-economic reality.

Now once this basic pattern of development–underdevelopment has been really grasped, much else, I would say all of the basic trends and tendencies of modern history, falls into place in a coherent and intelligible pattern. In the first place the absurdity of expecting or hoping that relations between the advanced and underdeveloped countries will result in the development of the latter becomes quite obvious. Trade, investment, government aid are precisely the means by which the advanced countries exploit the underdeveloped and maintain them in their underdeveloped condition. In the case of trade, this is fairly widely recognized. The exchange of raw materials for manufactured goods tends to reproduce and perpetuate itself, not to change into something else. And the tendency of import–export price relationships to move against the primary exporting countries in peace-time is notorious. There is absolutely nothing in the trade relationship as such tending to make for the development of the underdeveloping country – quite the contrary. The same is true of investment by the centre in the periphery, though this of course would be almost universally denied by the bourgeois economics profession. I do not want to try to enter into the intricacies of the theory of foreign investment, but I would like to call your attention to a few massive statistical facts which I suggest would be totally inexplicable if the relationship assumed by bourgeois economics were correct. I refer to the data on foreign investment of Britain and the US in their respectively two most active periods, which I think are conclusive on the effect of foreign investment in relation to the underdeveloped and developed areas.

The heyday of British imperialism and foreign investment, of course, was the half century before the First World War. In the period 1870–1913, according to the usually accepted figures, Britain invested abroad a net amount of 2.4 billion pounds. That is to say, the investment abroad by Britain exceeded the investment of foreigners in Britain by 2.4 billion pounds. At first glance, it looks as though Britain were making available out of its resources very substantial sums to the rest of the world. In fact it was a very substantial sum, about 12 billion contemporary dollars, and the purchasing power of the dollar was at least double what it is today: Thus, the net investment from Britain in the half century before the Second World War was around 25 billion dollars of our time. And that is a lot of investment by anybody's standards, then or now. But the catch, of course, is the other side of the coin – the income from this investment. And during the same period, 1873–1913, the net income from foreign investments to Britain amounted to 4.1 billion pounds. So that when you balance it out you find that the inflow on income account exceeded the outflow on investment account by roughly 70 per cent. That was the real flow of wealth for that period. It was going out with the right hand and coming in with the left, and the left-hand flow was about 70 per cent bigger than the right-hand flow. Who was aiding whom? Obviously the rest of the world, developed and underdeveloped, was paying tribute through this mechanism of investment to Great Britain.

Or take the experience of the US since the Second World War. I confine attention to direct foreign investment of US corporations, which in today's world is by far the most important type of foreign investment. Figures comparable to those which I have just cited for Britain, for the period 1950–63, are as follows: net outflow of capital from the US – 17.4 billion dollars; inflow of income to the US – 29.4 billion dollars. Once again it turns out that the inflow exceeded the outflow by almost exactly 70 per cent. I'm tempted to erect this into Sweezy's first law of foreign investment, that over any significant period of time the inflow from foreign investment will exceed the outflow of capital by 70 per cent. And I base that on good scientific procedure; I have at least two cases! And now I look for followers who will test and validate this law by every further case that becomes available.

Once again, we have to ask, who has been using whose wealth? And the answer is surely obvious.

Now as for what is somewhat comically called aid from the advanced to the underdeveloped countries, which is often pictured as the open sesame to economic development and all the rest, the record is all too clear, and here again we can formulate a law: the more aid, the less development. The reasons are numerous. A large part of the aid of course is military in nature, supposedly for defence against the bogy of communist aggression – though everyone over the age of ten knows that these subsidized military machines in the underdeveloped countries count for nothing in the world power-balance, and in reality serve only the purpose of propping up repressive governments in their own countries. But even more, most economic aid has nothing to do with development. Much of it goes into the pockets of corrupt local bureaucrats and officials, much of it is for the purpose of paying back debts and interest to the bankers of the country providing the supposed aid; and almost none of it is even intended for development. I'd like to quote a statement of a high official in the US foreign aid administrations under their various titles over the years, a man named D. A. Fitzgerald, who on his retirement from active service was interviewed by *US News and World Report*. Among other things, he said: 'A lot of the criticism of foreign aid is because the critic thought the objective was to get economic growth, and this was not the objective at all. The objective may have been to buy a base, or to get a favourable vote in the UN or to keep a nation from falling apart, or to keep some country from giving the Russians air base rights, any one of many other reasons.'

About the only other reason he does not mention is economic growth. The purpose, in other words, is obviously to preserve the status quo in which the underdeveloped countries go on underdeveloping, and the developed countries go on developing. Against this background I think the real meaning of the communist revolutions of the 20th century becomes clear. They are not, as bourgeois ideology would have us believe, some kind of historical accident which happened as a result of the chaos of wars or as a reaction to the ideological rantings of prophets by the name of

Marx and Lenin. Looked at in historical perspective, they are the result of an inevitable struggle of the underdeveloped countries to escape from the strait-jacket in which they have been entrapped for the last few centuries. Once caught in that system, the underdeveloped countries could only go on under-developing. Only outside of it could they start using their resources for their own purposes, could they start, in other words, a genuine process of economic development.

We now have plenty of examples of the contrast between what happens to countries inside and outside of the strait-jacket of the international capitalist system – countries which were, at the time of the escape of one and the continued imprisonment of the other, at roughly the same stage of development. China and India provide the most spectacular, and in the long run no doubt the most important, pair of countries, one of which is still imprisoned while the other has escaped. China is developing very rapidly by any standards, and in a rounded way – not the kind of lopsided development/underdevelopment reproducing pattern which is so characteristic of colonial countries. India, on the other hand, not only is developing internally in this uneven way but is hardly, on the average, advancing at all – statistics are not too reliable, but even the most optimistic show only a very small rate of increase of average per capita income; and of course, averages mean very little, the majority can easily be, and in the case of India probably is, actually losing ground. And now we see that starvation is beginning to become more or less endemic in various parts of the country and will undoubtedly spread in the years ahead.

The two Koreas are an equally impressive, if smaller scale, example. So are the two Vietnams. Although of course the picture in Vietnam is blurred by the massive intervention of the US, nevertheless, the pattern is clear – a significant, healthy development on the one side, and an incredible mess of underdevelopment and distortion on the other.

In the Western Hemisphere the contrast between Cuba on the one hand and the rest of Latin America on the other is equally striking and equally impressive. Everywhere we have the chance to make the comparison it seems to me that the lesson to be learned is unmistakable.

What conclusions are we to draw from this historical process of development-cum-underdevelopment? Is there any reality to this notion of the 'Great Contest' in which the underdeveloped countries are bidden to follow either the capitalist or the communist pattern? Is there any prospect that the advanced capitalist countries will be able somehow to pull themselves together and work out a programme which they can successfully apply to the underdeveloped countries? For my part, I think these are all pipe-dreams, whatever ideological dressing they come in, whether the liberalism of Washington or the peaceful co-existence of Moscow. The reality is that the underdeveloped countries are sentenced to death if they remain entrapped in the world capitalist system. And what ensures this, paradoxically enough, is the one export from the advanced capitalist world which has taken hold and been successful – the export of modern medical science, which has resulted of course in spectacular declines in death-rates (high as they still are in many parts of the underdeveloped world) without any corresponding increase in the capacity to produce, let alone the reality of production. So that you have what is commonly referred to as the population explosion, without anything developing alongside it to support it. It is a commonplace now that in another 30 or 40 years the population of the world will have doubled, pretty much regardless of what happens in that period to birthrates; and certainly well over half of this increase will take place in the underdeveloped countries. Certainly nobody in his right mind can imagine – and nobody does, really, who is at all well informed – that given the present institutional structures, the underdeveloped countries can feed, let alone raise the standards of nutrition, of that kind of a population growth.

Orville Freeman who is the US Secretary of Agriculture has warned that the 1970s will be 'a decade of hunger'. To that Fidel Castro replied in a speech last year: Freeman is wrong, the 1970s will be the decade of revolution. Because in the world today, people, whatever they may have done historically, would rather die from a bullet, says Fidel, than from the slow agony of starvation.

I believe that Fidel is telling the simple truth, and I do not see that there is the slightest prospect, given the present power structures, interest structures, institutional arrangements in the advanced capitalist countries, that there is anything they can or will do about it. I would not venture to predict exactly what forms these revolutions will take or how long they will be in developing. It may be, and I think myself very likely it will be, a whole historical epoch. It is even conceivable, because of the development of modern technology of destruction, that somewhere along the line the advanced capitalist countries, playing the role of Samson, will blow the whole world up and bring the process to an abrupt end. I would only add that if that should be the outcome, capitalism too would blow up. However you look at it, the future of the system is not a bright one.

Objective Values | *Paul Goodman*

Scientists, like other people, tend to notice what they are interested in. The hypothesis determines the experiment and what is salient has weight as evidence. But there is a problem special to the social sciences. The experimental part of social sciences is social action, finally political action; and when you engage in political action you have to get other people to co-operate with you. So what you notice, depending how you are in the world, must impose itself on the others and finally you must make them be, or see that they are, in the world in the same way.

Many of us are so extremely dissatisfied with the state of society that we want to change it structurally, make a revolution. But what we most want to change, and the lever that seems promising in order to make a change, is likely to differ from group to group, as each group is in the world. I trust that this is merely a commonsense remark. But my experience at this conference has been that when people disagree with me, one method they use to ignore me is to say, 'Oh that's just common sense.' And they then don't pay any attention to it and proceed as if it were not the case.

Let me discuss briefly three revolutionary crises as they appear to different groups. Start with one that is undebatable. There is a high risk that the world will be destroyed by nuclear war within the next ten or fifteen years, and everybody agrees that total destruction is a Bad Thing. Now if one has been, like myself, a pacifist for forty years, one is terribly impressed that during that period, since the First World War, the potentiality for destruction has been increasing at a rapid rate and has now reached catastrophic proportions. It follows quite simply from this that in the world at present the real We and They is the people of the world against the power structure of the world: the power is the enemy, whatever its politics or ideology. I don't mean necessarily that the different powerful nations are equally culpable politically or morally; but they are as powerful as they are because they think in certain terms. They have invested their capital and their brains along a certain line; for twenty years they have been stockpiling nuclear weapons or making desperate attempts to get them. Necessarily this kind of thinking becomes the rationality of their societies.

We can assume, I think, that no decision-maker plans for the bust-up, yet there is an almost inevitable drift towards that bust-up. And we can easily imagine circumstances that would produce it. Consider my own country. Suppose there is a continuing rash of very bad riots on the streets, and as a result an extreme reactionary group is swept into power. Then suppose that one of the big South American countries, Brazil or Chile, goes Castroite – as could happen at any time. It is almost inevitable that, in a panic, nuclear bombs would be dropped. I myself think that, *mutatis mutandis*, the same situation could occur in China within a few years (although many people at this conference would, of course, vehemently deny it). At present the Soviet bloc seems to be the balancing force of reason in the world, but I would not have said this in 1956 and who knows what the panic-level will be in 1976?

From this point of view, therefore, the immediate revolutionary slogan is 'Get the power away from the people who have that kind of power, whoever they are.' This involves getting rid of national boundaries, visas, censorship of international communication, Berlin walls. It means internationalizing space exploration, aid to underdeveloped regions, overseas youth corps, de-energizing national competition and building the world community. The notion of peaceful co-existence among national powers obviously does not work, for 'deterrence' is not a stalemate, it escalates.

The instinct of Gandhi was correct. So long as India was colonialized, he was a nationalist, for it was necessary first to find identity and shake off the imperial oppressor. But then, having achieved nationhood, it was wise to get rid of the Pakistan boundary and ultimately the Chinese boundary, to walk across those boundaries and make friends by the same non-violent means. So Buber in Israel. Buber felt, rightly or wrongly, that for historical reasons the Jews had to occupy Palestine and affirm their national identity with their own land. But then, once the State was established, he urged to dissolve it, to become bi-national and enter into fraternity with the Arabs at whatever cost, to spend the money sent by American Jews to create Arab–Israel co-operation. Gandhi and Buber were of course repudiated as entirely unrealistic, but who was realistic? Israel is now developing its atom bomb and India will develop an atom bomb if it has time.

In brief, during the national revolution it is necessary to keep in the back of one's mind that the only real revolution is humanity and peace. But to keep reconciliation in the back of one's mind is certainly injurious to one's rhetoric. It is a dilemma.

Two weeks ago I was in Hungary at an international meeting of youth leaders organized by the Friends. There were twenty young people from communist states and twenty from Spain, Italy, France, England, Holland, and the United States. In important respects it was clear that these young people had more in common with one another – a sub-culture of their own and an alienation from the incompetence, double-talk, and pressuring of the previous generation – than any had with their respective countries. They were, potentially, an international group of radical youth, with the same attitudes and slogans from New York or Madrid or Warsaw or Prague. (There were no Chinese present.) Finally, after they had adopted resolutions against the Vietnam war and on behalf of the French journalists in Bolivia, to test their temper I introduced the following resolution: Since there was an imminent threat of nuclear war, and since the older people were drifting, it was up to the young, just to survive, to take the issue into their own hands and form a common front transcending national and bloc boundaries. For instance, to organize co-ordinated demonstrations in all capitals against the great nuclear powers, and to try to boycott them. Especially the young of the non-nuclear nations could take the lead and try to sweep the others along.

This seemed to be an innocent proposal. I assured them that if we could get 500 picketing in Warsaw, we could get 50,000 in Washington. But at present, in America as in England, when the pacifist crowd grows to a certain point, there comes the cry, 'What about Them?', and this is hard to answer when there is nothing about Them.

What happened to the proposals? Except for two Maoists from Italy and a Trotskyist from England – I shall return to these – the young people from the West thought that it was a long shot but worth trying. The Yugoslavs supported it, as a common front, which they compared with the front against the Fascists in 1936. The young Czechs also were for it – intensely. (Indeed, when I tried to drop the matter since I could not get unanimity, they would not allow it, but went around trying to collect signatures.) They were, in fact, at daggers drawn with their own regime, which had censored their newspaper and was threatening to jail them. From the other communist countries I heard the following: The East Germans made the sad complaint, 'You are right but we do not dare demonstrate. We have suffered too much. You don't know what it's like.' The young Hungarian said, 'Foreign policy is the business of the government. If a youth group spontaneously initiates a demand on a point of foreign policy – even if it is the government policy – it is a subversive act. We are patriotic Soviet Hungarians.' The Poles were apparatchik types and accused me of bourgeois idealism, because I isolated the question of nuclear war from the general context of political conflict. The Italian Maoists and the English Trotskyist said that the present necessity was for China to develop an atom bomb and my proposal was divisive and counter-revolutionary. 'It would be better – I quote literally – 'that all mankind be destroyed than that 700 million Chinese be disadvantaged, for they are the future.'

I report this episode to illustrate the difficulties at present even of nuclear pacifism, even among radical youth.*

Turn now to the point of view of ecologists and community-planners, and a different revolutionary crisis seems salient: within a generation there will be a catastrophe because of the abuse of technology on an unprecedented scale, wrong land use, wrong urbanization, and over-centralized management. This crisis is understood mainly by professionals, biologists, engineers, educators, and psychiatrists, but it is felt universally as powerlessness, alienation, anomie, and in increasingly serious physical disasters and epidemic mental and social pathology. In some regions there is probably a real danger of over-population, though I tend to be sceptical of Malthusian arguments until glaring political and economic abuses have been remedied.

I won't spell out the sophisticated details of these environmental and ecological emergencies – others can do it far more competently and it is hardly any longer necessary, especially to people who live in giant cities. But the point is

*Finally the meeting adopted a simpler proposal: to establish a Committee of Correspondence on the subject, address Julian Lousada, 6 Rossetti Studios, Flood Street, London sw3, England.

that these things are going to do us in, maybe not so quickly as the atom bombs might, but maybe only ten years later if we are spared the bombs. But perhaps even more important is that because of the bad ecology, even in the present stage, the preparation or reconstruction of a decent society becomes less and less possible because of the ecological causes. Consider that the Mayor of New York has said that it would cost $50 billion to make New York 'livable'. There isn't going to be that kind of money; and what does it mean to live where it is unlivable and getting worse? to try to engage in reasonable politics when there is increasing alienation, anomie, depression, nervous disease, degenerative disease, overcrowding? Things might look fine on the surface – the Gross National Product might be rising in some places and in others everybody can be quoting from Chairman Mao's little red book, but all are getting deeper into the bog. Here again, clearly, we have to go across national, ideological, and bloc boundaries. But the relevant thinking – e.g. rural reconstruction, decentralization to countervail anomie, ecological education as more important than education for hardware technology – such things are not major political issues: they belong to crackpots.

It makes sloganeering difficult. How is one to say, 'Up with Chairman Mao' but 'Down with the Maoist educational system'? It is not impressive.

If you come from an ecological background, however, it will be self-evident to you that these considerations must be kept in the foreground. They are perhaps not *the* most important thing. But what *is* the most important thing?

Incidentally, I myself don't know how, politically, to handle this dilemma.

So let's turn quickly to another revolutionary situation which I guess everybody here would insist on as being pretty near to *the* most crucial thing: the fact that two thirds of mankind is getting relatively if not absolutely poorer because of the abuse of technology, economic greed, power plays and misguided foreign aid of the Have nations. This process certainly overrides the boundary between the so-called western nations and the so-called communist nations – though China is not yet a Have nation.

Now what do we find that the leaders of the majority of mankind, the defenceless and starving, do? They lust for the whole package of western technology. This is called their rising aspirations. The other day Stokely Carmichael was talking about African culture and the Africans following their own way; but in fact the political leaders were trained in Cambridge or Harvard or Moscow or the Sorbonne (where else would they be trained?); and the technicians have gotten corresponding high-technology training and, worst of all, the people themselves are childishly seduced by the wonders of the western standard of living.

The matter becomes desperate when the high-technology that is sought is armaments. For, the argument goes, 'unless we have dive bombers and ultimately atom bombs, we are defenceless, we are surrounded, we will be swamped and colonialized again'. This argument is true. But one must also say, then,

'You're in a dilemma. You aren't pursuing your own culture. Every step destroys your tribes, your way of life. The skills you had are lost, the new skills are beyond you in the foreseeable future. And the set-up is wildly inflationary. It requires an investment of $35,000 to employ one American workman. Your productivity, in world-market terms, is about one thousandth – though you used to feed your face. Necessarily you quit the farm, crowd the city, die of cholera. Etc., etc.'

Apparently all this – we are told by some – is best cured by dictatorships and big 'planning', a method by which it is certain that scores of millions will die.

A very few persons – the 'intermediate technology'

people, some people in the United Nations, people in various Peace Corps – try to solve the problem by being selective about the technology and using sophisticated science to tailor aid to local skills, resources, community patterns. Needless to say, this is not the thinking of those in political power. In Africa itself, so far as I have heard, the only one who is not in the bag is Nyerere of Tanzania – he seems to be making the attempt to start from where his people are and to take them on from there. I am told by Dave Dellinger, who knows Cuba well, that the Cubans also are finally beginning to try to withdraw from the power and market nexus disastrous to themselves and to ask, 'Who are we? How can *we* live well and happily and with increasing freedom?' If this is true, grand. But Tanzania and Cuba do not add up to an impressive fraction of the starving two thirds of the world.

Thinking in these terms, of the necessity of fairly immediate disarmament, the restoration of ecological balance, decentralized control, selective technological development, and so forth, I am clearly not in the revolutionary swim. These are not the matters that have been frantically discussed here. I do not think they will be much helped by power plays.

I am a kind of Jeffersonian, way out of date. In my opinion most political talk is much too ambitious. People expect to use political power to accomplish some excellence or grandeur. It cannot. What it can do, sometimes, is to guarantee a situation of minimum decency in which maybe something good will occur. From this point of view the good societies in the world at present are certainly small ones, perhaps Denmark, Tanzania, or so.

Consider Ireland. In my experience it is fairly decent. Priest-ridden as it is, its censorship is not intolerable – I have printed things in the *Irish Times* which I could not get in the London *Times* and certainly not in the *New York Times*. People are well fed because it is good farm country and, with all the backward agronomy and belief in leprechauns, it has not been ruined. Now the average national income in Ireland is just a fourth of the average in the United States. Yet it's absurd to say that one lives in Dublin only a fourth as well as in New York or Budapest. One lives quite as well, in some respects better, in some respects worse. Obviously something is wrong with the GNP way of looking at things.

To be sure the country is depopulating. This is partly, I guess, because of the priests, the mothers, and the sexual repression. A lively girl is certainly right to get out. Mainly, I suppose, it is because young fellows can't make any money, according to another standard. They are convinced that it *must* be better elsewhere where the money is, so they emigrate.

Even so, I feel that if we in the revolutionary movement had more modest aims, we would make more sense. Certainly the promise of technological advance was the simplification of relations with the environment and the enrichment of the quality of life; but instead it has given us complication of the environment and confusion of life.

Let me talk now about my own country. Because of justified anger and resentment, the speakers so far have slipped into a torturing of a Marxist explanation of the present American scene that really is irrelevant. To put it simply, we really go in less and less for old-fashioned exploitation: that is, we don't want surplus value from the Vietnamese and we don't want surplus value sweated from the hides of Negroes (though we did for 200 years). The present cash figures, however, tell a different – and worse – story. Our system gives out a continual subsidy to these peoples. In Vietnam it takes the curious form of building their infrastructure – e.g. large concrete air runways, and docks at which our marines disembark. These will no doubt last a long time and be among the biggest harbours in the world. Or consider a typical figure from Spanish Harlem, researched by one of the university seminars at Columbia. The city of New York, with Federal subsidies, pays out to each Puerto Rican family about $10,000 a year in special social services, welfare money, remedial reading, reform school for the delinquents, etc. A middle-class family a few blocks away doesn't get any of this. Now this is hardly exploitation of the poor in a classical sense; yet somehow none of the money gets to them in a usable way: it is rather a way of processing them, pushing them around, controlling their lives one way or another. And this is the vitally true meaning in the cry 'Black Power': not stop exploiting us, but give us the money to use our own way; get off our backs. Obviously, however, this is not explicable in terms of the older Marxist class struggle; it must be analysed in terms of a new concept of domination.

Consider a rough history of colonialism over the centuries and millennia. The oldest kind seems to be plain displacement and annihilation, as the Dorians descended into Greece and pushed out the Pelagians, or the Europeans pushed out the American Indians, with the slogan, 'Go away, die.' Next was the ancient colonialism whereby a strong group settled like an incubus on the older indigenous group and exacted tribute, with perhaps a little garrison left behind to collect the take. The next step, demanding a more complex technology, is to exploit the underdogs for their labour. Perhaps capital equipment is brought in, typically the sugar mills into Brazil or Cuba; the natives work for subsistence or less – this is the literal exaction of surplus value in Marxist terms. Or importantly, raw materials are exacted, processed back at home, and some of them then resold in the colony at a further profit – old-fashioned mercantilism. Needless to say, there is still a good deal of exploited labour in these last two senses, especially in Latin America, as John Gerassi pointed out.

Nevertheless, at present we can do without most of these imported raw materials sweated from the indigenous. In a pinch we do without them. Starting with the war shortages, for instance, we now mainly use artificial rubber. Our petroleum comes mostly from the United States, and with nuclear power we won't need much of it anyway. The metals give way increasingly to plastics, and the basic iron is home-dug. So this kind of domination of colonies is less and less important, though we keep it going to make the last buck.

But the peculiar character of modern domination is the following – and this applies both to the underdeveloped countries and to Harlem: The big powers want the other peoples simply to shut up, for those peoples do not belong to the lovely high technological system. They are unnecessary, we don't need their labour, we don't need their raw materials. Nor do they make interesting customers, since their economy is in a different league altogether. Unfortunately, when they begin to starve, they get rambunctious. Why don't they shut up and cease to exist? Frankly, the real inner policy of the US majority with regard to the Negroes is not racist at all; the Americans hold nothing against the Negroes, if only they would go in the middle of the Atlantic ocean and drown. This would be cheaper and more efficient for everybody. You see, this is a different story from the one that was told last week.

It is clearly the only possible explanation of the Vietnam war. We are asking, 'Why don't they go away? Is it possible that we have sent half a million troops there, and the very best new equipment – at $30 billion a year – and they still don't go away?' If they would finally go away, we could develop the rest of the world in a proper civilized style.

That is, we are back to the original, most primitive kind of colonialism, genocide.

In principle there are two kinds of technological expansion possible at present: in the case of somewhat backward peoples, like Canadians and Europeans, we give them capital and new equipment, so we can do business with them; in the case of very backward peoples who cannot be brought up to the market level, we must get them out of the way, so we can build the future.

Of course there are complexities. There are rival high technologies: the United States, France and Germany, Russia, Japan. And here there are alternative possibilities that create domestic friction in each of the giant powers. Contrast, in America, the Hawks and the Doves. On the one hand a lot of expansion of military high technology can occur by keeping the underdeveloped regions in being and fomenting wars in them, with rival groups supported by rival great powers. On the other hand (as the Chinese critics point out), some in the great powers think it would be wiser to create a new Congress of Vienna, especially by an *entente* of the United States and Russia, in order to have a general pacification and clear the decks for big progress. The principle of a Congress of Vienna is that nothing new is ever supposed to happen, ever, ever.

Unfortunately there is a third alternative that is still more likely in the foreseeable future, the dismal outcome predicted in Orwell's *1984* – a general world war among three or four great powers with shifting alliances. (Usually, in Orwell, these powers seem to be fighting about dividing up Africa.) One aspect of Orwell's novel, however, that makes it rather rosily romantic, is that his warring giants are not equipped with atom bombs.

Domestically the United States is an excluding society, in the sense that various styles and conditions of life become useless – though within the acceptable way of being a human being there is much social mobility.

We have noticed the exclusion of the Negroes and Spanish Americans, who comprise up to 12 or 13 per cent of the population. An even more important group – though not very much mentioned – is the farmers. The rural population is now about 5 per cent which means that 50 million must have been driven from the land during this century. This has purportedly been done in terms of efficiency and to take advantage of new technology, but of course the choice of technology and the concept of efficiency have been political decisions by dominant groups, chain-grocers, processors, etc. The aged are excluded at an increasingly early age. There are several million delinquent and insane who must be put away; but of course these are unacceptable only because of the standards and conditions of acceptability. Certainly more than 90 per cent of those who fill the big State mental institutions could be quite harmless to themselves or others in a different system of things. And very much of the delinquency was, in a simpler society, just vitality.

The greatest excluded group is the young (50 per cent of the population is under twenty-six). The school system is, by and large, a way of keeping the young on ice. Very little of it has any educational or vocational use; but all must be confined and processed in schools for at least twelve years, and more than 40 per cent of the older age group waste four more years in college. According to Edgar Friedenburg, one of our best sociologists of education, the chief use of the high schooling – whether the middle-class schools or the blackboard jungles – is to break the spirit.

Here again we must go beyond the classical Marxist interpretation of exploitation and class war. When John Gerassi said that the State can tolerate the Hippies because they are no threat to the structure, he was misinformed.

Proportionate to its numbers, this group is by far the most harassed, beat up, and jailed by the police. Negroes go scot free in comparison. The social response to the demonstrating Negroes is, primarily, 'Why don't they go away?' It is at the point of riot that deep anxiety begins to be aroused. But with the Hippies there is a gut reaction from the beginning – they are dirty, indecent, shiftless; they threaten the self-justification of the system.

For the psychology of the American system, the system of exclusion, is precisely to be puristic, squeamish, self-righteous, narrow in the options it allows; and, of course, intensely do-good and 'Humanitarian' in trying to get people to shape up. We have a very rich country and, quite the opposite of what Gerassi says, it can tolerate tremendous economic drains. It continually tries to buy people off. But it must buy them off in such a way that nothing really different can ever happen, that good order is preserved. As we anarchists say, however, this order is chaos. Therefore there are explosions.

What, then, can I and my friends suggest positively?

First, we are interested in what to do with the new technology – how to select it in the interests of prudence, safety, modesty, amenity, utility. For instance, which functions should be automated and which not? For sometimes it is of great human advantage to automate; in other cases it is dehumanizing and does not really perform the function promised. This is one of the profoundest questions we face, yet few are addressing it, and the pressure groups, both in the United States and elsewhere, are largely those who profit by automating ad lib.

Again, what functions should be protected from technological orginization altogether? Might it not be better in an advanced technological society if we protected all the children – let's say up to the age of thirteen – from intense processing – perhaps even to try to diminish old-fashioned socialization as much as possible? When structures are so fantastically complicated and hyperorganized there is a strong argument, for both happiness *and* efficiency, to try to protect the unorganized potentialities of life. Our tendency in schooling has been just the reverse, of course. Interestingly, Lenin was rather sold on progressive education, invited John Dewey to Russia, and so forth; but under Stalin and in the present managerial era, just as in the United States, processing has been intensified.

How, in technologizing a backward area, to minimize cultural takeover and disruption of community patterns? What fits local work habits, skills, materials? How to add technology in such a way that peoples can preserve their independence?

This leads to a second kind of question: how to extend liberty and democracy? Across the world – and here I agree with Ronnie Laing, though I wish he had said 'across the world' rather than merely 'in the United States' – a chief revolutionary need at present is to loosen the bonds of authority. Ronnie said that it is 'obedience' that will doom us. The Americans, I have been arguing, are far too obedient; Chairman Mao's readers certainly also look too obedient in the pictures. (Some might argue that the Chinese are obedient in a good cause, but I don't think that was Ronnie's point.) To loosen authority we certainly must loosen national and ideological loyalties. There must be a lot of decentralization of power and decision-making, in social organizations and industrial organizations. We must ask – and it is often an empirical question – where, how, and how much workmen can manage their own plants, children and teachers manage their own schools, loosed from the obedience syndrome. What is really efficient in the long run? Parliamentary democracy seems to have failed. So-called 'democratic centralism' obviously will not do.

Next I come to something that especially the young people don't want to hear. Most of these questions are professional questions, and it really is quite essential that people know something. Pure spirit, lively heart, courage, high aims are pre-requisite but not sufficient. Yet the young shun professionalism. And for good reason. Most professionals at present, certainly in the United States, are finks (in under-developed countries they tend to be incompetent bureaucrats), and the very idea of autonomous responsible professionalism has begun to fade; professionals are becoming nothing but personnel of organizations. They execute programmes handed down to them – no matter what; they do not criticize and reject the programmes in terms of their own best judgement and their ethical responsibilities.

Since they believe that to become a professional is to be corrupt and part of the hated system, many of the best youth quit school altogether to devote themselves to 'real' revolutionary activity, in the slums, and elsewhere. Some seem to think that in a good society there will be no professionals at all, no problems of health, engineering, or justice that require special competence. This is a sad dilemma. If they do not learn anything, these young will know nothing. In my opinion this attitude of theirs is a chief reason why they have so little positive programme for social reconstruction.

But when societies are badly functioning – and all the major societies are badly functioning – to be an authentic professional, or try to be, is itself revolutionary. It soon brings one into conflict; and since institutions are connected, one's conflict becomes general. The revolutionary spirit of an authentic professional is, perhaps, not hotly activist, but it is deeply committed, involves one's intimate habits, and is lasting.

What is needed is some kind of alliance between authentic professionals and the populism that is everywhere reviving. In this alliance the professionals must not lead or dictate. Power resides in the people; it comes 'from below'. In a complicated world, however, the ability to hire and fire their own professionals increases simple people's confidence in their own power. The professionals, in turn, must be professionally autonomous, not subject to short-range political aims and popular prejudices. Obviously this is a difficult relation, yet indispensable.

The young do not seem to want this coalition. Let me give two examples. I wrote a book called *The Community of Scholars*, at the end of which I made a proposal for the formation of a few tiny professional universities, to shock the big system. All that is required is ten professionals (mostly working in the world and not academics), and a hundred students; that is, the usual medieval university. This created apparent enthusiasm among the radical young and they began to carry out the plan in numerous 'free universities'. Yet in fact none of these has any professional or vocational content at all. They are devoted to 'Sensitivity Training', 'Freedom of Women', 'Castro's Cuba', 'The Psychedelic Experience'. These are no doubt fine things, but they are not at all what I had in mind.

Again, consider the tragic thing that has occurred in SNCC, excluding the white students. This has effectively cut SNCC off from potential professionals, since these good white students are the most promising authentic professionals. And SNCC provided a possible framework for the alliance of populism and authentic professionalism. Certainly SNCC is justified in its claim that Negroes must work out their own emancipation. Yet the reconstruction of society must in the end transcend separatism anyway.

Let me end with a remark about international action. At present, needless to say, there is no such thing as a working-class international; that ceased to exist in 1914. (We are now at the stage that the American CIO-AFL enthusiastically endorses the Vietnam war!) The one actual international in the world at present is the international of technology and management – that spreads its style and exchanges its persons right across the world. In every country it is mainly an abusive force, technology is abused, the methods of management are alienating. But it is the case that the Chinese physicists developing their atom bomb were trained in Caltech.

There is potentially another international, which I referred to at the beginning of this talk, the international of the young – the young people who have more in common with one another than with any of their own regimes; whether in Prague, or Warsaw, or Madrid, or Berkeley, they have a common danger, a common style, a common resentment. In my opinion this potential group is the only possible opponent of the present technical–managerial international. But to become so, it must learn something and push for the right use of technology, the liberating method of management.

Criticism and Dogmatism
in Literature | *Lucien Goldmann*
(*Translated by Ilona Halberstadt*)

I must admit that when I arrived I did not have a very clear picture of the nature of this conference and I felt some apprehension at having proposed to speak on a literary topic at a gathering which seemed interested primarily in psychiatry and social and political problems. But on reflection it seems to me that my subject is not completely out of place, for two reasons:

1. I approach literary creation from a perspective which treats it not as an irrational and mysterious phenomenon, the result of the extraordinary inspiration of a genius separated from other men and from ordinary life, but on the contrary as a particularly precise and coherent expression of the problems which pose themselves to ordinary men in their daily lives and of the ways in which they are led to resolve them. Thus when I speak of the function of the critical spirit and of dogmatism in literary creation, I am speaking ultimately of problems closely related to those which confront all of us in the various spheres of our social, economic and political life.

So that, by dwelling to a certain extent on the bond between cultural creation and daily life, my speech can easily be related to your work as a whole.

2. However, in addition to this general reason, the second reason relates specifically to recent developments in Western societies. It seems to me that when we try to think seriously and critically, avoiding dogma and prejudice, about the situation of man in the advanced industrial societies (which, we must always remind ourselves, constitute only one part of the globe, but nevertheless have their own particular and

specific problems), we will discover that more than at any other time in history, and more than anywhere else in the world, the problem of attaining consciousness and of giving it expression (of which cultural and literary action constitutes only one part) has today assumed an importance that is decisive – or at any rate decisive in a different way than it was say at the time when Marx elaborated his theoretical thought.

I think that today we should distinguish two sectors, or if you prefer, two different blocs in the ensemble of Marx's classic analyses. One of these seems to me to have lost its validity to a great extent, at least with regard to industrial societies, and therefore must be appreciably modified. It consists of that set of analyses which deal with immiseration, the increasing poverty of the great majority of the members of society, and the fact that given such immiseration and poverty, the proletariat must, if not inevitably, at least very probably, attain revolutionary consciousness.

If we really wish to understand the social reality in which we live, it is time that we grasp the fact that real historical evolution has followed a course very different from that which Marx predicted and expected. Today the industrial world constitutes (from this viewpoint, and only from this viewpoint) a privileged sector in which the working classes of a number of countries have been integrated to a certain extent into global societies, so that to continue to speak of immiseration, of increasing poverty and of the revolutionary orientation of the proletariat is quite simply to think and live a myth. It is nonetheless true that things are far from ideal or even acceptable in these societies. Although they have assumed new forms, the problems of man, of his development and of liberation, remain desperately serious. This does not alter the fact that all this sector of Marx's analysis appears outmoded today, even if it was valid in the second half of the nineteenth century. It is certain that the problem of the liberation of man and of hopes for the future no longer poses itself for us at this level. It should be unnecessary to recall that 'for us' refers here to all the members of industrial societies and that in the whole of the Third World the problem of poverty has maintained its anguished primacy.

The other sector of Marx's analyses has, on the contrary, not only preserved its validity but appears much more relevant today than it was in Marx's time: this is the well-known analysis of reification. Here Marx showed that already in liberal capitalist society, relations between men had lost much of their qualitative and human character and had been transformed into mere quantitative relations. Moreover, their essence as social and interpersonal relations disappeared from man's consciousness to reappear in a reified form as a property of things. For example with regards to relations between the participants in the various stages of production of a finished product their co-operation disappears from their consciousness and is now only expressed in a property of commodities, namely price. This establishes in the market the only link between the stock-breeder, the dealer in skins, the tanner, the cobbler or the manufacturer of shoes, the retailer and the consumer. This situation results in the fundamental deformation of the individual, which is expressed on very different levels. One of the most important manifestations of this is the fact that in capitalist societies an individual is split into two or three parts: the citizen, the actor in economic or professional life, and the private individual. In each of these sectors he has different values and rules of conduct and he is not able to realize unity in his life or a harmonious development of his personality.

Thus today, in comparison with the nineteenth century, this process of distortion and stifling of the human personality has reached a much more advanced stage. For –

and my friend Marcuse has given us remarkable analyses of this phenomenon – with the development of that which has been variously called the consumer society, planned capitalism, organizational capitalism, or mass production society, even the individual's autonomy, which was still a reality in liberal society (at least for the middle and governing classes), is in the process of being eroded and of disappearing. In liberal society, reification consisted above all in the disappearance from consciousness of the superindividual social totality in favour of an individualism – illusory no doubt in as far as it aspired to be absolute, but nevertheless partly real. Today, with the exception of a few extremely limited ruling circles, man, the individual, finds progressively fewer sectors of social life in which he can still have initiative and responsibility. He becomes more and more a being who is only asked to carry out decisions taken elsewhere and who is given in return a guarantee of possibilities of increased consumption. This situation implies a narrowing and a dangerous and considerable impoverishment of his personality.

Let us add that this is a process which is as yet only in its infancy and which threatens to assume greater proportions to the extent that organizational capitalism develops. Although mass production already operates in many spheres today, and ranges over all sorts of goods (refrigerators, cars, etc.), nevertheless the true mass product or organizational capitalism, the one whose production, perhaps as yet quite limited, threatens to develop in the future, is the specialist who is simultaneously illiterate and a graduate of a university. This is a man who is very familiar with one field of production and has high professional qualifications to carry out in a satisfactory and even remarkable manner the tasks which are assigned to him, but who is increasingly losing all contact with the rest of human life, and whose personality is thus being deformed and narrowed to an extreme degree. The title itself of Marcuse's remarkable work, *One-Dimensional Man*, expresses in three words the most important problem posed in our societies for those concerned with the possibilities of leading a human life and with the implications of the very theme of our Congress: the dialectics of liberation.

This contraction of the human personality peculiar to organizational capitalism, which will continue to increase if social development maintains its present direction, is the result of the action of society on the most diverse levels and which I do not have the time to analyse in detail today.

First of all there is the influence of man's real social and economic life which in our society is constituted above all by the conjunction of three elements:

1. the increasingly specialized behaviour of the agent;
2. the disappearance of responsibility;
3. the rising standard of living and the possibilities of increased consumption.

The existence of the third factor, of course, facilitates the acceptance of the two others as well as a mental adaptation to existing society. This adaptation is also largely the effect of a whole range of intellectual actions which sociologists who have studied mass communications and the way in which information is transmitted in industrial societies exposed some time ago.

This is why, if we ask today what the possibilities are for counteracting the tendencies of social evolution, of giving a different direction to this evolution, and of defending man's freedom and the hopes for society which would assure him the possibilities of authentic development, there is a precise answer: action must be carried out on the level of social and economic reality and on the level of consciousness. For action which is social and economic alone can always be shaped by the mental and intellectual influence of the existing society on its members. This is frequently the case in most of the countries we are talking about, where the dominant strata succeed in deflecting the discontents of the workers and even of cadres – and I refer here to the analyses of Marcuse, Mallet and Gorz – preventing people from becoming conscious of the fact that their discontent is not only situated at the level of consumption and income, but that behind this lies another malaise, more vague, perhaps, but more general; a maladjustment of the human structure to a social reality which does not allow it to express itself and to develop. So ultimately the conflict can be resolved and the individuals integrated by conceding them a slightly higher income and an improvement of their material situation.

But all purely cultural action is also condemned in advance if it does not rest on a reality, or at least on social and economic action which allows men to maintain and even to develop mental structures favouring the comprehension of their condition and an attainment of consciousness. It is the great discovery of the Yugoslav socialists that one cannot fight against bureaucracy without counterposing to it social and economic structures with anti-bureaucratic tendencies, notably 'workers' control'.

However, our societies have a structure and a past too different from Yugoslav society to allow us simply to adopt the ideas of Yugoslav socialists. We therefore have to ask ourselves what possibilities there are for a reorientation towards a social order which would guarantee to men true responsibility and real participation in decision-making. In Western societies, workers' control is a basic perspective which is no doubt important and seductive. But it has no immediate prospects, and I do not think that we can develop it without formulating the demand for 'co-determination' as an intermediary stage.

But if this is true about social and political action, there still remains the other side of the coin, the possibility of creating the mental conditions which would permit the members of our societies to understand this programme and this perspective.

In effect, the struggle for participation in decisions and responsibilities, for 'co-determination' as a stage towards the workers' control of economic and social life appears to me to be the only course of action which would lead to the conditions of life in which workers could assimilate and live authentically the cultural reality which humanist intellectuals, scholars, writers and philosophers strive to transmit to them. But at the same time – and this is the theme of my speech – the problems of consciousness and its development become more important than ever in the struggle for a truly human society. That is why a study of the conditions of the development of consciousness and its links with real life have a place among the problems we are discussing here.

After these general considerations I would like to divide my speech into two sections: the first, relatively brief, in which I shall speak of the structure of knowledge in general and of the function of dogmatic and critical elements; the second devoted to the specific conditions of literary creation which, as I shall try to demonstrate, are analogous to the general conditions of attaining consciousness.

In a genetic and dialectical epistemology, consciousness and its development are of course separated from the rest of the life of man, but since one would need more than a year's course of lectures to explain dialectical epistemology as a whole, I will content myself with enumerating a few ideas of particular importance:

1. One of the merits of dialectical thought has been to show that the creative subject of all intellectual and cultural life is social and not individual. Every time we study either a historical event or the masterpieces of the history of literature and the philosophy of art, we find that the subject, that

active and structured unity which makes possible a significant account of the action of men or of the nature and meaning of the work which we are studying, is not an individual but a superindividual reality, a human group.

Nor is this subject the sum of a number of individuals, but rather a specific social group, standing, of course, in opposition to other groups, but also acting together with the groups to which it is opposed, and, within this opposition, acting on nature. I believe that this constitutes one of the most important differences of any dialectical sociology from positivist thought, which still sees objective reality as constituted by immediate, isolated and partial facts, and sees individuals as the subjects of historical behaviour and creation.

To avoid any misunderstanding one must, however, specify that the collective subject exists only within the limits of historical cultural action, and that there is also a sector of human life which has an individual subject, the one which Freud explored and designated as the realm of the *libido*. I am far from denying the reality and place of this realm in men's lives, but I believe (and here I express one of my most important reservations regarding a whole part of Freud's work) that the *libido* and libidinal behaviour do not provide a valid explanation of the meaning of any historical creation or of any cultural creation. For one cannot reduce the significance in general of a valid work of art, an authentic philosophical thought, or a historical creation, to individual desire. Freud has analysed the conflict between individual desires and the demands of society in a remarkable way; but I consider that he gave too much emphasis to the first, and that in men's lives it is the collective subject which allows the understanding of the sense and genesis of all that is historical and, implicitly, of that sector of historical life which is constituted by culture and cultural creation.

I shall now have to be a little more abstract and complex

in raising a problem which must eventually be thrashed out with the psychiatrists in the discussions which follow. I believe that the French philosophical tradition, from Descartes to Sartre, has been too much a philosophy of consciousness in general and, specifically, of individual consciousness, and that it has not explained or even considered a fundamental aspect of reality: this is that reason and meaning already exist at the biological level (for example, a cat who is hungry and catches a mouse exhibits perfectly meaningful behaviour which can be translated in terms of a problem and a solution of the problem); further that even on the human level, when consciousness does appear with its corollaries, language and communication, it is no doubt a crucial and inevitable element, but one element only of the not fully conscious meaning of collective behaviour. The result of this is – putting aside certain modifications which I do not have time to elaborate here* – that a great difference between psychoanalytic explanation and dialectical explanation and understanding arises at this point: both are genetic structuralisms, both start with the idea that all human behaviour is meaningful and that its meaning is grasped only partially at the conscious level; and both try to illuminate this significance. However, when a psychoanalyst explains a dream or a delusion he can only make it meaningful by relating it to the unconscious and by incorporating the latter into the structure which is released. Even after having been analysed, a dream and a delusion never become significant if we restrict ourselves to their manifest content. The psychoanalyst cannot interpret them without accounting for them, without linking them to the unconscious desires of the individual.

* On this subject see my article regarding 'Le Sujet de la création' (the subject of creation), *Revue de Sociologie de l'Université de Montréal*, No. 1, and *L'Homme et la Société*, No. 6 (Ed. Anthropos, Paris).

But if we pass on to history and to the relation of historical events or cultural works to the superindividual subject, we find ourselves in a related, but different situation. No doubt in the works of Racine, Malraux or Genet there are meanings or elements of meanings of which their authors were not aware; but once the analysis has been completed, the work (if it is sufficiently valid, i.e. has enough historical reality) appears as having a meaning in itself which can be illuminated without invoking any external or explanatory element.

This is because, at the level of collective action, consciousness is an essential phenomenon with *relative* autonomy; i.e. constituting – especially in the privileged cases of great cultural works and great historical events – a structure meaningful in itself and *relatively* autonomous. On the contrary at the level of the *libido*, though consciousness doubtless intervenes (since the behaviour of men living in society always has a partially conscious aspect), libidinal behaviour remains biological, analogous (though more complex) to that of the asocial animal (the cat of which we just spoke, for example), for which the conscious element never constitutes a meaningful and relatively autonomous structure as such.

So that in research it is only at the social level that we can clearly distinguish between internal *comprehension* on the one hand – demonstration of a structure which explains most of any event and (as in my own researches) almost the whole of a literary text – and on the other hand *explanation* which is the demonstration of the functional relation between such meaning and the behaviour of a collective subject.

2. I turn now to the two elements which are the subject of this speech: dogmatism and the critical spirit. I will first examine the normal and healthy structure of thought (later, of literary creation), a structure from which, through the

excess of one or other of these elements, often develop the social and intellectual pathologies which are dogmatism and a purely critical and negative spirit.

In so far as men's consciousness is an element of their action on the world, on nature and on other men, it is always bound *to introduce order* in the infinite diversity of sensations and signals which reach it from the external world. One cannot act without introducing a stable and enduring element, a constant, into the continuous, permanent flow of sensations. This applies at all levels of reflection, of attaining consciousness, and primarily at the simple level of the constitution of the object. When I say that there is a 'glass' here, this glass as such is not a simple datum of the external world, but consists of a creation of the human mind, a constant; the object, which introduces order and relative permanence, is a set of sensations in continual flux. (These sensations are not the same at noon and evening, or when we look from the left or the right, and yet we always speak of the same glass.) There is a children's joke which poses the problem in a relevant way; it concerns Johnny who explains to his friends that his father has an extraordinary knife which he has kept for forty years. Every two years he changes the blade, and in alternate years the handle! Under these conditions what is Johnny's father's knife? Is it a permanent and durable reality? Certainly not; a simple word? Not that either; rather it is a concept which permits a set of signals which come from the external world to be ordered and transformed into information, opening the way for praxis and behaviour.

If we now turn to the most general level we can establish that in order to live and orientate themselves men have always been obliged to introduce a more or less conscious order into their total picture of the world; and that all groups tend to build a picture similar to that which we have called, when speaking of privileged groups that constitute the agents of cultural creation, a *world vision*. Of course, these creations of mental categories and of pictures of the universe which, I repeat, go from the constitution of objects, across the principles of conservation in the sciences (conservation of energy, matter, etc.) to the total pictures which human groups construct of relations between men and between man and the universe, are not valid except to the extent that, beginning with a concrete situation, they succeed in making empirical reality intelligible and giving direction to behaviour. It is nonetheless true that no effective action is conceivable without such ordering.

At the level of the attainment of consciousness of the world, of mental categories, we must assert, as Hegel and Marx have demonstrated to us, that global structurations of categories have only temporary value. They are generally valid for certain specific social groups in a certain concrete historical situation, but to the extent to which – through the very action of men who use them as jumping off points, or through external influences – the world is transformed and situations change, mental categories cease to be efficacious, lose their rationality and must transform themselves in turn. This is why the same world views, the same modes of thought which were valid and allowed men to live and act in a particular epoch become dogmatic in relation to a changed reality which they no longer fit.

Dogmatism becomes pathological and morbid to the extent that, in defending certain ideas and positions, ordering and attitudes in a situation which no longer corresponds to them, it is favouring the preservation of ancient privilege and institutions and opposing the action of men who aspire to freedom. And it is to this same extent that a critique of all dogmatism is valid, urgent and justified. But one must not fall into the opposite extreme and forget that the ordering of the world, the creation of constants, the elaboration of theoretical thought is absolutely essential in order that men may live, orientate themselves and act efficaciously.

That is why it is impossible to content oneself merely with the critical spirit, the second element of all consciousness and all healthy theoretical thought. I shall now speak about this.

One of the most important ideas in dialectical philosophy is that thought is always an attempt to discover a meaning in life under certain concrete conditions and to establish a praxis which will tend to change reality in the direction of the hopes of human groups; moreover this behaviour as a whole always demands a living synthesis between the rational ordering mind, on the one hand, and the application of the critical spirit to reality on the other.

Now all order has hitherto implied sacrifices and repressions (although it may one day cease to do so). Marx on one level, Freud on another, and many others since, have shown us this. First of all there is repression in the sphere of the adaptation of the individual, of his *libido*, his aspirations, his desires, to social reality. It is true that this repression does not always have the same intensity or the same breadth, and one of the problems which must arise when one reflects upon the dialectics of liberation concerns the possibilities of creating a social order which would assure the minimum of repression of individual aspirations for happiness, as well as an equitable distribution among the various social classes of the sacrifices entailed by these repressions. Yet it is no less important to know that up till now all social order, all attempts of action in history to subdue nature, to develop culture, to create a technology, to organize social and human relations, have always implied a certain number of decisive sacrifices of the aspirations of the individual. The most elementary example is that of the prohibition of incest, which is found in almost all human societies. Since the appearance of society the prohibition of incest seems to have been a primary condition of its continuing to exist without dissolving into small self-enclosed groups.

In addition to this example, and to all the repressions and suppressions which any society imposes on its members, there is also a great deal of repression based on the privileges which a ruling minority appropriate within a given social order, imposing on the masses the sacrifices which correspond to the minority's privileges. Each of these types of repression must of course be closely studied by those who are concerned with the problems of human freedom. It is very important to remember that, even if a certain number of sacrifices imposed on the oppressed groups appear necessary at certain times in order to assure the progress of society as a whole, there always comes a moment when modifications in the social situation render these sacrifices superfluous and open the way for the demand for their abolition.

Thus situations occur where the retention of repression no longer corresponds to any necessity of society as a whole and serves solely to perpetuate outmoded privileges. One must therefore always have a clear perception of the fact that all order – even though it appears to be rational, reasonable and even desirable at a certain point of time – carries with it sacrifices, and that these sacrifices must be accepted only in a very provisional way up till the moment when it becomes possible to abolish them.

At the same time, one needs to distinguish carefully what at any given moment remains a painful but justified and inevitable necessity, from outmoded and irrational privilege and dogmatism which manages to maintain itself only with the help of those whom it favours and in the absence of comprehension and of consciousness on the part of those whom it oppresses.

The critical spirit, then, is absolutely necessary, not only in the obvious sense that it may encourage the actual liberation of all that is merely a dogmatic survival from the past, but also because it retains its necessity and function even in the face of a necessary and rational dogmatism, since it must create the actual conditions for the subsequent transcendence of that dogmatism and for future liberation.

Moreover, if there is a pathology of dogmatism, there is also a corresponding pathology of the critical spirit. This consists in forgetting that criticism must always be formulated in relation to the existing possibilities of men in a given situation, to the needs and demands of praxis, and that it must never become unilateral by ignoring the ineluctable necessity for ordering. The dialectical spirit is above all the attempt to maintain the two opposed extremities of the chain while always remaining on guard against the deformations which can go in one direction or the other.

Taking up the problems of literary creation, I would like you to recall that all my works are based on a definition of art and aesthetic value which was basically formulated for the first time by Kant and which is found again, with modifications and qualifications, in Hegel and then in all Marxist literary aesthetics. The valid work of art is defined as a transcendence, on a non-conceptual level, of the tension between extreme unity and extreme complexity; between on the one hand the variety of a complex imaginary universe and on the other hand the unity and rigour of creation. You can see straight away how these two elements, these two poles, if you like, of the work of art, correspond on the aesthetic level to that which I have called in epistemological analysis the critical element and the dogmatic element. To this very general and historical Kantian definition, Hegel later brought a major qualification: that unity is not always the same but depends on the particular historical epoch. Finally, genetic structuralism has replaced the purely intellectual Hegelian historicity by concrete and positive history in which intellectual unity is always functionally related to the evolution of the totality of the social structure.

If I now examine the works of literary criticism inspired by the Lukacsian school to which I subscribe, I would say that, while admitting in principle the position that I have outlined, the disciples of this school have felt compelled to demonstrate scientifically and positively, in a certain number of specific instances, the unity of the work of art, the world vision to which it corresponds, and the relations between this world vision and the social groups (notably the social classes) of which it is an expression. If I take as an example my own case, I can say that first of all I confined myself to showing the existence of unitary and coherent world visions around which the works of Racine, Pascal, Malraux and Genet revolve.

The reasons for this fundamentally somewhat unilateral approach were that it appeared to be both the most urgent and the most difficult task, given that erudite university criticism, be it impressionist or thematic, at best uncovered in the world of the work of art certain elements of richness and complexity, but entirely neglected, indeed never really tried to isolate seriously, its unity by taking into consideration the wholeness of the text. But in giving this explanation of our attitude I am perhaps being optimistic, for one cannot exclude the possibility that the privileged place which we gave to the unity of the work of art at the expense of the place given to the complexity and richness of its universe may have been affected by the predominance of dogmatism during the whole period of the history of Marxist thought. Even if this was the case, we are dealing of course with an implicit and unintentional connexion, for on the explicit level, not only I myself but most of the other scholars of this orientation have defended the critical spirit and have clearly and explicitly opposed all dogmatism. Whatever the case may be, it remains true that in consecrating most of our efforts to the unity of the work of art and to the relation between this unity and the consciousness of certain social groups, we neglected in effect the richness and complexity of the world of the work of art, even if we never ceased to recognize its importance. For this recognition was much more a matter of principle than of fact, and at bottom we probably thought that richness attached itself primarily to the individuality of the writer and could not be approached from a sociological perspective. Moreover, in this we were giving in to a prejudice firmly established in university criticism.

In the analyses of which I speak, I think I have shown that contrary to psychoanalytic work, which reveals the action in dreams or delusions of individual desires opposing the social structure, cultural creation achieves a unity and a coherence which favour the development of collective consciousness; in sum, literary creation has among its other functions that of helping the group to become conscious of its problems and of its aspirations, while on the contrary the dream or the delusion act against such attainment of consciousness and attempt to shape it through sublimation and symbolism (for the attainment of consciousness is important in analysis only in so far as it aims to avoid maladaptations and to resolve problems which arise in pathological situations).

It seems to me, however, that at the very level of this attainment of collective consciousness there exists a constitutive element which forms part of every authentic and valid work of art and which we have neglected too much. It is not sufficient to state in principle that the works of Racine, Pascal or Molière are great because they introduce a unified rigorous structuration into a rich and complex world. One must study this richness concretely and uncover that which the work of art affirms as sacrifice, a sacrifice indubitably necessary to the order which the work represents and recognizes as valid, but which nonetheless remains a sacrifice and a limitation. In the long run it is that element of the work which is related to the necessity of the critical spirit, and which by this very fact indicates the possibility of hope for the future, which will be able to transcend the very order which it defends today.

Of course such analyses must have a concrete character and must deal with particular works, or particular writers. But this constitutes a programme of work for the future. Today, I would simply like, following some studies which have just appeared, to indicate three sectors towards which I feel research of this kind must be orientated. It seems to me that in these sectors the critical function forms a constitutive element of every important literary work, an element through which are expressed not only the actual aspirations of a privileged social group but also the hope of transcending one day these aspirations in favour of a vaster and more humane order.

Using as a model an article by Julia Kristeva on Bakhtine,* I think the sectors are as follows:

1. A social and cultural domain whose exploration in any case belongs to the field of the sociology of culture. All great literary work carries a unitary world vision which organizes its universe (I have demonstrated this elsewhere). For the work of art to be truly great, one must however be able to find in it also an awareness of values rejected and even repressed by the vision which makes up the unity of the work, and an awareness of the sacrifices which men have to suffer because of the refusal and repression of these values. It may very well be possible that Racine condemns unilateral and exclusive passion, but one cannot understand the greatness of Racine's work if one does not perceive the degree to which it carries an understanding of the humane function of such passion, of its possible value and the loss to mankind which follows from its refusal. The fact that in *Le Misanthrope* Molière rejects Jansenism is incontestable, and

* *Critique*, No. 239, 1967.

we have tried to show the degree to which this condemnation was justified in the perspective of the group to which he gave voice (in this particular case, the court nobility). But it is not any the less important, for the purpose of understanding the play, to see the degree to which Molière expressed there a human value of absolute spirit, and the limitation which the defence of good sense imposes on men in refusing to integrate a character of Alceste's greatness into their midst.

2. Another realm, no longer of a sociological but of an ontological nature, is also on the side of variety as opposed to unity: we have already said that any world vision has a functional relation to certain privileged social groups, in that it is a means of helping these social groups to live and to manipulate the problems which arise in their relations with other social groups and with nature. In doing this, however, every world vision comes up against an ontological reality which it cannot subdue: that of death. That is why it is important, when studying the structure of a philosophy or a work of art in a valid manner, to ask oneself in what way it has resolved or at least come to terms with its confrontation with this fundamental reality of human existence (for example, by ignoring it, by integrating it into the hopes of survival of the collectivity or in the hopes of individual survival, or by putting it at the very centre of the attainment of consciousness).

3. Finally, there is the realm of conflict between the individual's aspirations and the social order, the reality of the sacrifices which every order exacts at the level of individual existence. For if, as I think, criticism inspired by psychoanalysis has been incorrect in trying to place individual aspirations at the origin of cultural creation itself, it remains true nevertheless that cultural and particularly literary creation (even though it expresses the unity and collective rigour of group aspirations) implies a more or less acute

awareness of the sacrifices which the group aspirations exact at the level of the individual's existence. The *libido* thus constitutes an important element in the work of art, not from the point of view of unity and coherence, as the psychoanalysts believe, but on the contrary from the point of view of the complexity and richness which stand opposed to structuration.

Allow me to end this speech with a critical remark about my latest book. In the chapter devoted to the *nouveau roman*, to the works of Robbe-Grillet and of Nathalie Sarraute, I still insisted, as in my previous analyses, on the unity of their works, on their realistic character, and on the fact that they help us to understand the world in which we live. For example, I showed that *Les Gommes* by Robbe-Grillet transposes into an imaginary world one of the fundamental mechanisms of contemporary society and of organizational capitalism: economic and social self-regulation; that *Le Voyeur* centres on the passivity of men which is one of the fundamental facts of contemporary industrial societies; that *La Jalousie* centres on reification, and so on. I tried in that study to show, in face of a number of opponents of the *nouveau roman*, the degree to which these writings carried a realistic, critical and perfectly coherent vision of contemporary society, and the degree to which their imaginary universe made them into valid and authentic literary works.

I was criticized for this – and at the time I was adamant, but today I think that the objection was valid – because of what was called in general terms the poverty and dryness of the genre. For it is true that while the unity of these works is rigorous, the other pole, the integration in the unity itself of the very possibilities and potentialities of human reality of which it is unaware or whose sacrifice it requires, occupies in these works a relatively small place. Let us take as an example Robbe-Grillet's first novel, *Les Gommes*. It is the story of a group of murderers who get rid every month of any one individual, in this actual instance an individual called Dupont. One day they make a mistake and a Dupont escapes them. The self-regulation of the universe functions, however, in such a rigorous manner that by the end of the book the character who is conducting an investigation into the imaginary murder of Dupont, which yet lacks a Dupont as victim, ends by actually killing Dupont in such a way that order is re-established and the murderers can go on to kill the next Dupont. The transposition of self-regulation into an imaginary world is rigorous, but the whole story is told without any anguish, without any condemnation, and one cannot find in it even a rough sketch of the possibility which this universe refuses and denies, the possibility of another world in which equally powerful forces could direct the Duponts not to death but to life, and even to a more authentic and rich life.

That is why I am inclined to think today, even if we do find within this genre representative and authentic literary works, that they express nevertheless a general impoverishment of literary and cultural creation. This impoverishment is analogous and parallel to that which Herbert Marcuse has highlighted as a general characteristic of the contemporary capitalist world by establishing that, of the two dimensions of existence, the actual and the possible, which characterize man, the possible, on which the essence of literary creation rests, is increasingly tending to disappear from men's consciousness, producing in the end what he calls 'the one-dimensional man'.

The contraction of the dimension of the possible implies without doubt a considerable impoverishment in the field in which cultural creation develops. It is not adequate, however, to establish and to assert this, for the problem is only in a small way that of the will and talent of the writers. It is rather the problem of the status of man in modern society, of which cultural creation forms an important but only a single part.

Thus it is in fighting for the transformation of this global reality, for the widening of the realm of the possible, both on the level of participation in responsibilities and in decisions, and on that of thought and consciousness, that we can perhaps contribute one day to a reorientation of the actual evolution of society. This is the only basis of hope for a freer mankind and a more authentic culture which are fundamentally only two aspects of one and the same problem and which will one day in the future become, let us hope, two aspects of one and the same reality.

We had intended to prepare a written speech for this Congress, and had started to prepare it three weeks before the trip, but the US government thought that as I was starving it would be better if they saw to it that I got some meals every day, so they confined me to their prison system, and I lost all the notes. So I tried to get another one together.

Now since I've been at the Congress from Saturday I've been very confused, because I'm not a psychologist or a psychiatrist, I'm a political activist and I don't deal with the individual. I think it's a cop out when people talk about the individual. What we're talking about around the US today, and I believe around the Third World, is the system of international white supremacy coupled with international capitalism. And we're out to smash that system. And people who see themselves as part of that system are going to be smashed with it – or we're going to be smashed.

So that I'm not going to centre on the individual – I'm not even going to talk about him at all. I want to talk about the system. I want to use some quotes to back up my feeling about talking of the system, and the first one comes from one of my patron saints: Frantz Fanon. His quote is that

Freud insisted that the individual factor be taken into account through psychoanalysis. It will be seen that the black man's alienation is not an individual question. It is a question of socio-diagnostics. The Negro problem does not resolve itself into the problem of Negroes living among white men, but rather of Negroes exploited, enslaved, despised by the colonialist, capitalist society that is only accidentally white.

But since it is accidentally white, that's what we talk about – white western society.

Now the other reason that I don't talk about the individual is that I feel that whenever you raise questions about racial problems to white western society, each white man says 'Well don't blame me, I'm only one person and I really don't feel that way. Actually I have nothing against you, I see you as an equal. You're just as good as I am – almost.' And to try and clear that up I want to point out the difference between individual racism as opposed to institutionalized racism.

It is important to this discussion of racism to make a distinction between the two types: individual racism and institutional racism. The first type consists of overt acts by individuals, with usually the immediate result of the death of victims, or the traumatic and violent destruction of property. This type can be recorded on TV cameras and can frequently be observed in the process of commission.

The second type is less overt, far more subtle, less identifiable in terms of specific individuals committing the acts, but is no less destructive of human life. The second type is more the overall operation of established and respected forces in the society, and thus does not receive the condemnation that the first type receives.

Let me give you an example of the first type: When unidentified white terrorists bomb a black church and kill five black children, that is an act of individual racism, widely deplored by most segments of the world. But when in that same city, Birmingham, Alabama, not five but 500 black babies die each year because of lack of proper food, shelter and medical facilities; and thousands more are destroyed and maimed physically, emotionally and intellectually because of conditions of poverty and discrimination in the black community, that is a function of institutionalized racism. When a black family moves into a home in a white neighbourhood, and it is stoned, burned or routed out, the latter is an overt act of individual racism, and many people condemn that, in words at least. But it is institutionalized racism that keeps the black people locked in dilapidated slums, tenements, where they must live out their daily lives subject to the prey of exploiting slum landlords, merchants, loan-sharks and the restrictive practices of real-estate agents. We're talking now about the US, but I think you can apply a little of it to London. But the society either pretends it does not know of institutionalized racism, or is incapable of doing anything meaningful about the conditions of institutionalized racism. And the resistance to doing anything meaningful about institutionalized racism stems from the fact that western society enjoys its luxury from institutionalized racism, and therefore, were it to end institutionalized racism, it would in fact destroy itself.

O.K. then, now I want to talk about de-mystifying human beings, and I'm talking about the Third World, I'm not talking about the white West. I think that the Third World are the people whom, at least in the US, black people are concerned with. The white West has been able to do very well for itself. I want to talk, then, very specifically about a number of things under that.

The first is the importance of definitions. The second: we want to talk about cultural integrity versus cultural imposition. And then we want to talk about the US, specifically the cities and the rebellions (as opposed to 'riots' as they are called by the white press) that are occurring in the US, which are going to lead to guerrilla warfare. And we want to talk about violence because the West is always upset by violence when a black man uses it. Yeah.

I want to start off with definitions by using a quote from one of my favourite books, which is *Alice in Wonderland*, by Lewis Carroll. In the book there's a debate between

Humpty Dumpty and Alice around the question of definitions. It goes like this:

'When I use a word,' Humpty Dumpty said, in a rather scornful tone, 'It means just what I choose it to mean. Neither more nor less.'

'The question is,' said Alice, 'whether you can make words mean so many different things.'

'The question is,' said Humpty Dumpty, 'who is to be master. That is all.'

Now I think that Lewis Carroll is correct. Those who can define are the masters. And white western society has been able to define, and that's why she has been the master. And we want to follow up with a lot of those examples, because I think that the white youth of my generation in the West today does not understand his own subconscious racism, because he accepts the writings of the West, which has destroyed, distorted and lied about history, so that he starts off with a basic assumption of superiority which is not even recognizable.

Frederick Douglas, the great black leader of the 1800s, said that when a slave stops obeying a master, then and only then does he seek his liberation. Camus said the same thing 100 years later on the first page of *The Rebel*, when he said that when a slave stops accepting definitions imposed upon him by his master, then and only then does he begin to move and create a life for himself. That's very important, because what the people of the Third World are going to have to do today is to stop accepting the definitions imposed on them by the West. Let's give some examples.

The first one is that the history books tell you that nothing happens until a white man comes along. If you ask any white person who discovered America, they'll tell you 'Christopher Columbus'. And if you ask them who discovered China, they'll tell you 'Marco Polo'. And if you ask them, as I used to be told in the West Indies, I was not discovered until Sir Walter Raleigh needed pitch lake for his ship, and he came along and found me and said 'Whup – I have discovered you.' And my history began.

But let us examine the racism in that statement. Let us examine it very closely. Columbus did not discover America. Columbus may be the first recorded white man to have set foot in America. That is all. There were people there before Columbus. Unfortunately, those people were not white – unfortunately for the white West, fortunately for us, they weren't white. But what happens is that white western society never recognizes the existence of non-white people, either consciously or subconsciously. So that all around the world, the peoples of the Third World never did anything until some white man came along – and that's why China's non-existent, because Mao won't let no white folk in there. Yeah. And pretty soon Hong Kong is going to be non-existent because they're going to kick them out.

So that the situation you have is that history has been written – but indeed it has been so distorted. One of the biggest lies, I think, that western society could have told was to name itself Western Civilization. And now all through history we were studying Western Civilization, and that meant that all else was uncivilized. And white kids who read that today never recognize that they're being told that they are superior to everybody else because they have produced civilization. At best, that's a misnomer, at worst, and more correctly, it's a damn lie. Yes. Western Civilization has been anything but civilized. It has been most barbaric, as a matter of fact. We are told that Western Civilization begins with the Greeks, and the epitome of that is Alexander the Great. The only thing that I can remember about Alexander the Great was that at age twenty-six he wept because there were no other people to kill, murder and plunder. And that is the epitome of Western Civilization. And if you're not satisfied with that, you could always take the Roman

Empire. Their favourite pastime was watching men kill each other or lions eating up men. They were a civilized people. The fact is that their civilization, as they called it, stemmed from the fact that they oppressed other peoples. And that the oppression of other people allowed them a certain luxury, at the expense of those other people. That has been interpreted as 'civilization' for the West, and that is precisely what it has done. The only difference is that after the Roman Empire, when the British Empire – on which the sun never used to set, but today it sets, sometimes it don't even rise – began to exploit non-white people, what they did was they let colour be the sole choice of the people they would exploit.

Now that's very important because as we go along you can see one of the best examples you can see today. You see, because you've been able to lie about terms, you've been able to call people like Cecil Rhodes a philanthropist, when in fact he was a murderer, a rapist, a plunderer and a thief. But you call Cecil Rhodes a philanthropist because what he did was that after he stole our diamonds and our gold, he gave us some crumbs so that we can go to school and become just like you. And that was called philanthropy. But we are renaming it: the place is no longer called Rhodesia, it is called Zimbabwe, that's its proper name. And Cecil Rhodes is no longer a philanthropist, he's known to be a thief – you can keep your Rhodes Scholars, we don't want the money that came from the sweat of our people.

Now let us move on to present times. I'm always appalled when some white person tells me that 'progress is being made'. I always ask him 'progress for whom? And from whom?' Progress for white people might be made, because I would say that since World War II they have learned a little about how to get along with people of colour. But I don't think there's been progress for the black people, there's not been progress for the people of colour around the Third World. And progress will not be measured for us by white people. We will have to tell you when progress is being made. You cannot tell us when progress is being made, because progress for us means getting you off our backs, and that's the only progress that we can see.

Now then, we want to talk about cultural integrity versus cultural imposition, because that stems from definitions. Because the white West felt somehow that it was better than everybody else – I remember when I was a young man in the West Indies, I had to read Rudyard Kipling's *The White Man's Burden*. I thought the best thing the white man could do for me was to leave me alone, but Rudyard Kipling told them to come and save me because I was half savage, half child. It was very white of him. What has happened is that the West has used force to impose its culture on the Third World wherever it has been. If a few settlers left England to go to Zimbabwe, there was no reason for them to rename that country after themselves, Rhodesia, and then force everybody to speak their language, English. If they had respect for the cultures of other people, they would have spoken the language of those people and adopted their religions. But what in fact happened was because the West was so powerful – that's the word nobody wants to talk about, power. It was only power that made people bow their heads to the West, you know. They didn't bow it because they liked Jesus Christ, or because they liked white folks. No, Machiavelli said a long time ago that 'people obey masters for one of two reasons. Either they love them, or they fear them.' I often ask myself whether or not the West believes the Third World really loves them and that's why they've obeyed them. But it's clear that they feared them. The West with its guns and its power and its might came into Africa, Asia, Latin America and the USA and raped it. And while they raped it they used beautiful terms. They told the Indians 'We're civilizing you, and we're taming the West. And if you won't be civilized, we'll kill you.' So they committed genocide and stole the land, and put the Indians on reservations, and they said that they had civilized the country.

They weren't satisfied with that. They came to Africa and stole Africans and brought them to the USA, and we were being brought there to be 'civilized', because we were cannibals and we ate each other, and they were going to give us a better life, which was, of course, slavery.

Now I want to make just one clear distinction, before I move on, in terms of cultural integrity. Inside the countries of the West there was democracy for the whites, at least some form of it. But that democracy was at the expense of non-white people. While Britain surely enjoyed her papers, and her Parliamentary nonsense about constitutionality, she was suppressing all of Africa. The same thing holds true for France, and De Gaulle still suppresses Somaliland, I would like to inform him; and the same thing, of course, is true today for the US.

White people are very funny, you know. De Gaulle got out of Vietnam a few years ago, and now he's gotten very broad-minded. But he's still in Somaliland.

So what the West was able to do is impose its culture and it told everyone 'we are better, we are civilized'. And because of its force, all of the non-white countries began to try to imitate Europe and to imitate its ways, and to try and copy it because nobody wanted to be uncivilized. . . . Our ancestors had recognized that they knew what civilization was long before Europeans even got out of their caves, and that they should have stuck to their way of life. Had they done that, perhaps we shouldn't be in the shape we are in today.

So that all other non-western people have been stripped of their own culture. They have been forced to accept a culture that does not belong to them. And so messed up are the minds of people of colour around the world, that in certain sections of Vietnam today, and in Japan certainly, women who have slanted eyes are cutting their eyes so that they can get round eyes to look like the West. Needless to say what black people have been doing to their hair, especially females: they have been putting hot combs in their hair, straightening it, attempting to look like white people, because the West has defined beauty as that which was theirs – the white woman, who was supposed to be taboo.

And so the non-white world began to copy and to imitate, began to do all of the things of the West. I think what is happening in the world today is that there's a fight for cultural integrity. Each group of people wants to retain its own integrity, and say 'To Hell with the West and its culture. Let it keep it. We want ours.' I don't propose to speak for the Red Guards, but I would assume that that's part of the fight that they're waging. It's a healthy fight and it needs to be waged. I know in the US that one of the fights that we're waging is the fight for our own cultural integrity. We want to be able to recognize the contributions that the non-white peoples of the world have made. It's amazing that, when you do some reading, you find out that they did most of what the white people claim that they did. They just distorted history. Pythagoras didn't give you geometry, the Egyptians gave it to you.

I have something against England, I really do. Because when I was young I had to read all that rot about how good England was to Trinidad, while she was raping us left and right. And all I used to read about London when I was small was the beauty of London, and how peacefully everybody lived, and how nice life was – at my expense. And I used to say 'I sure would like to get to London and burn it down to the ground.' But that's violence!

Now the trouble with the West is that it feels it has the right to *give* everybody their independence. That's totally absurd. You can never *give* anyone their independence. All men are born free. They are enslaved by other men. So that the only act that the men who enslaved them can do is, not give them their independence, but stop oppressing them. There's a very important difference, and I don't think people make that distinction all the time. I'm amazed when I pick up the paper and read that 'England today decided to give independence to the West Indies.' Who the hell is England to give me my independence? All they can do is stop oppressing me, get off my back. But it sounds so much nicer when they say, 'We're giving you your independence. You're ready for it now.' Rather than for them to admit to themselves 'We're going to stop oppressing you because we're becoming a little bit more civilized; or because you're making it uncomfortable for us and we can no longer afford to oppress you at the price that you're asking us to pay.' Which is correct. But you wouldn't expect self-condemnation.

So that you cannot grant anybody independence, they just take it. And that is what white America is going to learn. They cannot *give* us anything. No white liberal can give me anything. The only thing a white liberal can do for me is to help civilize other whites, because they need to be civilized.

Now in order to move on to the US – because I know what's on everybody's mind is the rebellions and the guerrilla warfare that is taking place inside the US – I'd just like to read some of the notes that I jotted down, so that you can maybe get a clearer picture, because you don't live in the States. However, I don't think you really need that much of a clearer picture, because England isn't far behind.

It is estimated that in another five to ten years two thirds of the 20 million black people that inhabit the US will be living in the ghettoes, in the heart of the cities. Joining us are going to be hundreds of thousands of Puerto Ricans, Mexican Americans, and people of the American Indian population. The American city, in essence, is going to be populated by the peoples of the Third World while the white middle classes will flee to the suburbs. Now the black people do not control, nor do we own, the resources – we do not control the land, the houses or the stores. These are all owned by whites who live outside the community. These are very real colonies, in the sense that there is cheap labour exploited by those who live outside the cities. It is white power that makes the laws, and enforces those laws with guns and sticks in the hands of white racist policemen and their black mercenaries. It does not seem that at any point the men who control the power and resources of the US ever sat down and designed those black enclaves, and formally articulated the terms of their colonial and dependent status, as was done, for example, by the Apartheid government of South Africa which both Britain and the US and France backs. Yet one cannot distinguish between one ghetto and another as one moves around the US. It appears as if each ghetto is the same. Note that the US has, within its continental borders, forty-eight states, and each of these states has a ghetto in all of its major cities. As one moves from city to city it is as though some malignant, racist, planning unit had done precisely this : designed each one from the same master blue-print. And indeed, if the ghetto had been formally and deliberately planned, instead of growing spontaneously and inevitably from the racist functionings of the various institutions that combine to make the society, it would somehow be less frightening. The situation would be less frightening, because if these ghettoes were the result of design and conspiracy, one could understand their similarity as being artificially and consciously imposed, rather than the result of identical patterns of white racism which repeat themselves in cities as far apart as Boston is from Watts – that is, 3,000 miles.

We understand that a capitalist system automatically contains within itself racism, whether by design or not. Capitalism and racism seem to go hand in hand. The struggle for Black Power in the US, and certainly the world, is the struggle to free these colonies from external domination. But we do not seek merely to create communities where, in place of white rulers, black rulers control the lives of black masses, and where black money goes into a few black pockets. We want to see it go into the communal pocket. The society we seek to build among black people is not an oppressive capitalist society. Capitalism, by its very nature, cannot create structures free from exploitation.

The question may be asked, how does the struggle to free these internal colonies relate to the struggle against imperialism all around the world? We realistically survey our numbers and know that it is not possible for black people to take over the whole country militarily. In a highly industrialized nation the struggle is different. The heart of production and the heart of trade is in the cities. *We* are in the cities. We can become, and are becoming, a disruptive force in the flow of services, goods and capital. While we disrupt internally and aim for the eye of the octopus, we are hoping that our brothers are disrupting externally to sever the tentacles of the US.

That's very important, because Newark, New Jersey, is where Engelhart has his capital – and for the last five days he couldn't do any work. Good move for the Africans. You know who Engelhart is, don't you – you don't – you should read about South Africa, he controls most of it, along with Rockefeller, the liberal from the US.

It is sometimes said that the African–American movement in the US does not understand the true nature of the struggle in the world today; that the movement is involved in fighting only racial discrimination, and only with the weapon of non-violence. It used to be. As you know, the Black Power movement which SNCC initiated moved away from the movement for integration. This was not only because the movement's goals were middle class – such as job opportunities for college graduates, equal public facilities – and not only because white Americans' concept of integration was based on the assumption that there was nothing of value in the black community and that little of value would ever come from the black community – and that's very important, because the West doesn't understand its own racism when they talk about integration. When they talk about integration, they talk about accepting black people – isn't that ridiculous? I have to talk about whether or not I want to accept *them*, and they're never willing to talk about that, because they know they'll come up losing. So that integration is absolutely absurd unless you can talk about it on a two-way streak, where black people sit down and decide about integration. That means if you're really going to talk about integration, you don't talk about black people moving into white neighbourhoods, you talk about white people moving into black neighbourhoods.

Because of the middle-class orientation of the integration movement, and because of its subconscious racism, and because of its non-violent approach, it has never been able to involve the black proletariat. It could never attract and hold the young bloods who clearly understood the savagery of white America, and who were ready to meet it with armed resistance. It is the young bloods who contain especially the hatred Che Guevera speaks of when he says, and I quote:

'Hatred as an element of the struggle, relentless hatred of the enemy that impels us over and beyond the natural limitations of man, and transforms us into effective, violent, selected and cold killing machines.'

The Black Power movement has been the catalyst for the bringing together of these young bloods – the real revolutionary proletariat, ready to fight by any means necessary for the liberation of our people.

The Black Power movement in the US is exposing the extent of the racism and exploitation which permeates all the institutions in the country. It has unique appeal to young black students on campuses across the US. These students have been deluded by the fiction in white America that if the black man would educate himself and behave himself, he would be acceptable enough to leave the ranks of the oppressed and have tea with the Queen. However, this year, when provoked by savage white policemen, students on many campuses fought back, whereas before they had accepted these incidents without rebellion. As students are a part of these rebellions, they begin to acquire a resistance-consciousness. They begin to realize that white America might let a very few of them escape, one by one, into the mainstream of a society, but as soon as blacks move in concert around their blackness she will reply with the fury which reveals her true racist nature.

It is necessary, then, to understand that our analysis of the US and international capitalism is one that begins in race. Colour and culture were, and are, key factors in our oppression. Therefore our analysis of history and our economic analysis are rooted in these concepts. Our historical analysis for example views the US as being conceived in racism. Although the first settlers themselves were escaping from oppression, and although their armed uprising against their mother country was around the aggravation of colonialism, and their slogan was 'no taxation without representation', the white European settlers could not extend their lofty theories of democracy to the red men, whom they systematically exterminated as they expanded into the territory of the country which belonged to the red men. Indeed, in the same town in which the settlers set up their model of government based on the theory of representative democracy, the first slaves were brought from Africa. In the writings of the glorious Constitution, guaranteeing 'life, liberty, the pursuit of happiness' and all that other garbage, these were rights for white men only, for the black man was counted only as three fifths of a person. If you read the US Constitution, you will see that this clause is still in there to this very day – that the black man was three fifths of a man.

It was because white America needed cheap or free labour that she raped our African homeland of millions of black people. Because we were black and considered inferior by white Americans and Europeans, our enslavement was justified and rationalized by the so-called white Christians, who attempted to explain their crimes by spouting lies about civilizing the heathens, pagans, savages from Africa, whom they portrayed as being 'better off' in the Americas than they were in their homeland. These circumstances laid the systematic base and framework for the racism which has become institutionalized in white American society.

In our economic analysis, our interpretation of Marx comes not only from his writing, but, as we see it, from the relationship of capitalistic countries to people of colour around the world. Now I'm going to use the Labour Movement as an example to show what happens when people in a white country in the West organize themselves when they're being oppressed. I want to use the Labour Movement in the US because it's always quoted around the world as the real movement, or friend, of the black man, who is going to be able to help him. This is true for all other little white countries when the white workers organize – here's how they get out of the bind.

The Labour Movement of the US – while in the beginning certainly some of their great leaders in the struggle were against the absolute control of the economy by the industrial lords – essentially fought only for money. And that has been the fight of white workers in the West. The fight for one thing – more money. Those few who had visions of extending the fight for workers' control of production never succeeded in transmitting their entire vision to the rank and file. The Labour Movement found itself asking the industrial lords, not to give up their control, but merely to pass out a few more of the fruits of this control. Thereby did the US anticipate the prophecy of Marx, and avoided the inevitable class struggle within the country by expanding into the Third World and exploiting the resources and slave labour of people of colour. Britain, France, did the same thing. US capitalists never cut down on their domestic profits to share with the workers. Instead, they expanded internationally, and threw the bones of their profits to the American working class, who lapped them up. The American working class enjoys the fruits of the labours of the Third World workers. The proletariat has become the Third World, and the bourgeoisie is white western society.

And to show how that works – and not only how it works just in terms of the bourgeoisie – I've watched the relationships of whites to whites who are communist, and whites to non-whites whom they call communist. Now every time the US wants to take somebody's country, they get up and say 'Communists are invading them and terrorist guerrilla warfare is on the way, and we must protect democracy, so send thousands of troops to Vietnam to kill the Communists.' Italy is a white country. Over one third of its population is communist. Why doesn't the US invade Italy? Tito is an acknowledged communist. The US gives him aid. Why don't they invade Tito's country, if they really care about stopping communism? The US is not kidding anybody. When they want to take over somebody's land who is non-white, they talk about communist aggression – that's what they did in Cuba, in Santo Domingo, and it's what they're doing in Vietnam. They're always telling people how they're going to stop them from going communist. And don't talk about dictatorship. Franco is perhaps the worst dictator in the world today, but the US gives him aid.

So that it is clear it is not a question of communist invasion; it's really a question of being able to take the countries they want most from the people, and the countries they want most are obviously the non-white countries because that is where the resources of the world are today. That's where they have been for the last few centuries. And that's why white western society has to be there.

Now we want to make two distinctions, because when rebellions break out in the large cities of America, the first thing that people say is that they're riots. And white western society is very good, the first thing they want is order; law and order. 'We must have law and order.' They never talk about justice, because they're incapable of talking about it. Hitler had the most efficient system of law and order I've ever seen. He happened to have been a fascist. He did not have justice coupled with his law and order. The US knows about law and order, it doesn't know about justice. It is for white western society to talk about law and order. It is for the Third World to talk about justice.

Now we want to talk just a little about violence. For God's sake, I don't understand how the white West can ever talk against violence. They are the most violent people on the face of the earth. They have used violence to get everything they have. And yet they're the first to talk against violence. The armed rebellions and the guerrilla warfare going on in the US today is not the most violent thing going on in the world. Vietnam, South Africa, Zimbabwe, Hong Kong, Aden, Somaliland – that's where your violence really is. For violence takes many forms. It can take the form of physical warfare, or it can take the form of a slow death.

The Jews in the Warsaw ghettoes were suffering from violence. It didn't take an actual physical form until they were put in the gas chambers, but they were suffering from mental violence. Wherever you go in Africa today, the Africans are suffering from violence, violence inflicted on them by the white West, be it that they are stripped of their culture, of their human dignity, or of the resources of their very land.

And it is crystal clear to the peoples of the Third World today that it's time out for talk. There can be no talk about how to stop violence. That's clear because even Camus talks about that, even though he cops out. Camus talks about executioner/victim. He says, well, there's executioner/victim relationships in society, and the executioner uses force to keep his victim down. But the victim gets tired of that. And what happens is that when the victim moves either to a position of equality or to try to conquer the executioner, he uses the force and the means and the methods that his oppressor used to keep him down. That happens to be violence. I never get caught up with violence. As a matter of fact, one of my favourite quotes on that, to stop all the talk about it, is a quote from Sartre, which my patron saint used. Sartre says:

What then did you expect when you unbound the gag that had muted those black mouths? That they would chant your praises? Did you think that when those heads that our fathers had forcefully bowed down to the ground were raised again, you would find adoration in their eyes?

That's Jean-Paul Sartre, not me.

We are working to increase the revolutionary consciousness of black people in America to join with the Third World. Whether or not violence is used is not decided by us, it is decided by the white West. We are fighting a political warfare. Politics is war without violence. War is politics with violence. The white West will make the decision on how they want the political war to be fought. We are not any longer going to bow our heads to any white man. If he touches one black man in the US, he is going to go to war with every black man in the US.

We are going to extend our fight internationally and we are going to hook up with the Third World. It is the only salvation – we are fighting to save our humanity. We are indeed fighting to save the humanity of the world, which the West has failed miserably in being able to preserve. And the fight must be waged from the Third World. There will be new speakers. They will be Che, they will be Mao, they will be Fanon. You can have Rousseau, you can have Marx, you can even have the great libertarian John Stuart Mill.

I want to tell you why violence is important in terms of building a resistance-consciousness in the US. Now I want to use a quote which we learned from Germany:

The triumph of the Storm Troopers required that the tortured victim allow himself to be led to the gallows without protesting, that he repudiate and abandon himself to the point where he ceases to affirm his identity.

There is nothing more terrible than these processions of human beings going to their death like human beings. I'm afraid black Americans cannot afford to march to the gallows the way Jews did. If the US, white America, decides to play Nazis, we're going to let them know the black Americans are not Jews, we're going to fight back to the death. And in case you think that sounds very violent, let me remind you of a poem that your great, great Prime Minister, Sir Winston Churchill, read when you were getting ready to attack Germany, even though you were told that you were a minority. He read a poem, incidentally, I don't know if he told you, which was written by a black man named Claude McKay from Jamaica, and he wrote it for black people. It is called 'If we must die'. It is our poem today in the US. Its message goes something like this:

'We will nobly die, fighting back, and for each of the thousand blows we will deal one death blow. But we're going to die like men. We are not going to take the oppression of white society any longer. That is clear in our minds. How it is in white society's mind is another question, but they are not defining for us any longer our struggle. We will define our struggle and we will carry it out as we see fit.'

We have to extend our fight internationally, not only because such a consciousness would destroy within black communities the minority complex so carefully calculated by the American press, but also because we know that if the black man realizes that the counter-insurgency efforts of the US are directed against his brothers, he will not fight in any of their wars. He will not go. Then it will become crystal clear to the world that the imperialist wars of the US are nothing less than racist wars. During the past year we have initiated a black resistance movement to the Draft, which is being led by our hero, the World Champion, Mr Mohammed Ali. Not only because we're against black men fighting their brothers in Vietnam, but also because we're certain that the next Vietnam will either be in the Congo, in South Africa, in Zimbabwe, Bolivia, in Guatemala, in Brazil, in Peru, or indeed in the West Indies. And we are not going to fight our brothers.

And to answer your question about violence, the African-American has tried for the past 400 years to peacefully co-exist inside the US. It has been to no avail. We have never lynched a white man, we have never burned their churches, we have never bombed their houses, we have never beaten them in the streets. I wish we could say the same for white people around the world. Our history demonstrates that the reward for trying to peacefully coexist has been the physical and psychological murder of our peoples. We have been lynched, our houses have been bombed, and our churches burned. We are now being shot down like dogs in the streets by white racist policemen. We can no longer accept this oppression without retribution. We understand that as we expand our resistance, and internationalize the consciousness of our people, as our martyred brother Malcolm X did, we will get retaliation from the government, as he did. As the resistance struggle escalates we are well aware of the reality of Che's words, when he says:

'The struggle will not be a mere street fight, but it will be a long and harsh struggle.'

And to the end, we are going to work with our common brothers and sisters in the Third World to fight this oppression.

I would like to conclude, then, by telling you just precisely what black people in America are going to do, and when we're going to do it, and how we're going to do it, and why we're going to do it. This is your only chance to hear it clear, because you'll be hearing it from the BBC next time.

Black people in the US have no time to play nice polite parlour games, especially when the lives of our children are at stake. Some white Americans can afford to speak softly, tread lightly, employ the soft sell and put-off – or is it putdown? – because they own the society. For black people to adopt their methods of relieving our oppression is certainly ludicrous. We blacks must respond in our own way, on our own terms, in a manner which fits our temperaments. The definition of ourselves, the road we pursue, the goals we seek are our responsibility. It is crystal clear that society is capable of, and willing to, reward those individuals who do not forcefully condemn it – to reward them with prestige, status and material benefits. But these crumbs of corruption will be rejected. The plain fact is that as a people we have absolutely nothing to lose by refusing to play such games. Anything less than clarity, honesty and forcefulness per-

petuates the centuries of sliding over, dressing up and sooth-
ing down the true feelings, hopes and demands of an oppressed black people. Mild demands and hypocritical
smiles mislead white America into thinking that all is fine
and peaceful; they lead white America into thinking that
the path and pace chosen to deal with racial problems are
acceptable to the masses of black Americans. It is far better
to speak forcefully and truthfully. Only when one's true
self, black or white, is exposed can society proceed to deal
with the problems from a position of clarity, and not from
one of misunderstanding.

Thus we have no intention of engaging in the rather
meaningless language so common to discussions of race in
the world today. They say:

'Things were and are bad, but we are making progress.
Granted, your demands are legitimate, but we cannot move
hastily. Stable societies are best built slowly. Be careful that
you do not anger or alienate your white allies. Remember,
after all, you are only ten per cent of the population.'

We reject the language and these views, whether expressed by blacks or by whites. We leave them to others to
mouth, because we don't feel that this rhetoric is either
relevant or useful. Rather we suggest a more meaningful
language – that of Frederick Douglas, a great black
man who understood the nature of protest in society. He
said:

Those who profess to favour freedom, yet deprecate agita-
tion, are men who want crops without ploughing up the
ground. They want rain without thunder and lightning. They
want the ocean without the awful wrath of its many waters.
Power concedes nothing without demands – it never did and
it never will. Find out just what any people will quietly submit
to, and you have found out the exact measure of injustice and
wrong which will be imposed upon them. And these will continue until they are resisted with either words or blows, or with

both. The limits of tyrants are prescribed by the endurance of those whom they oppress.

He was a slave.

Black Power, to us, means that black people see themselves as a part of a new force, sometimes called the Third World; that we see our struggle as closely related to liberation struggles around the world. We must hook up with these struggles. We must, for example, ask ourselves: when black people in Africa begin to storm Johannesburg, what will be the reaction of the US? What will be the role of the West, and what will be the role of black people living inside the US? It seems inevitable that the US will move to protect its financial interests in South Africa, which means protecting the white rule in South Africa, as England has already done. Black people in the US have the responsibility to oppose, and if not to oppose, certainly to neutralize the effort by white America. This is but one example of many such situations which have already arisen around the world; there are more to come.

There is only one place for black Americans in these struggles, and that is on the side of the Third World.

Now I want to draw two conclusions. I want to give a quote from Fanon. Frantz Fanon in *The Wretched of the Earth* puts forth clearly the reasons for this, and the relationships of the concept called Black Power to the concept of a new force in the world. This is Mr Fanon's quote:

Let us decide not to imitate Europe. Let us try to create the whole man, whom Europe has been incapable of bringing to triumphant birth. Two centuries ago a former European colony decided to catch up with Europe. It succeeded so well that the USA became a monster in which the taints, the sickness and the inhumanity of Europe has grown to appalling dimensions. The Third World today faces Europe like a colossal mass, whose aim should be to try to resolve the problems to which Europe has not been able to find the answers. It is a question of the Third World starting a new history of man, a history which will have regard to the sometimes prodigious thesis which Europe has put forward, but which will also not forget Europe's crimes, of which the most horrible was committed in the heart of man and consisted of the pathological tearing apart of his functions and the crumbling away of his unity.

No, there is no question of a return to nature. It is simply a very concrete question of not dragging men towards mutilation, of not imposing upon the brain rhythms which very quickly obliterate it and wreck it. The pretext of catching up must not be used for pushing men around, to tear him away from himself or from his privacy, to break and to kill him.

No, we do not want to catch up with anyone. What we want to do is go forward all the time, night and day, in the company of man, in the company of all men.

Since there's been a lot of talk about psychology, I've thought up a psychological problem. White liberals are always saying 'What can we do?' I mean they're always coming to help black people. And I thought of an analogy. If you were walking down the street and a man had a gun on another man – let's say both of them were white – and you had to help somebody, whom would you help? It's obvious to me that if I were walking down the street, and a man had a gun on another man, and I was going to help, I'd help the man who didn't have the gun, if the man who had the gun was just pulling the gun on the other man for no apparent reason – if he was just going to rob him or shoot him because he didn't like him. The only way I could help is either to get a gun and shoot the man with the gun, or join the fellow who doesn't have a gun and both of us gang up on the man with the gun. But white liberals never do that. When the man has the gun, they walk around him and they come to the victim, and they say 'Can I help you?'. And what they mean is 'help you adjust to the situation with the man who has the gun on you'.

So that if indeed white liberals are going to help, their

only job is to get the gun from the man and talk to him, because he is in fact the sick man. The black man is not the sick man, it is the white man who is sick, he's the one who picked up the gun first.

So the psychologists ought to stop investigating and examining people of colour, they ought to investigate and examine their own corrupt society. That's where they belong. And once they are able to do that, then maybe we can move on to build in the Third World.

I want to conclude, then, by reading a poem that was written by a young man who works in SNCC, the organization for which I work. His name is Worth Long. It's called 'Arson and Cold Grace, or How I Yearn to Burn, Baby, Burn'.

We have found you out, four faced Americans, we have found
    you out.
We have found you out, false faced farmers, we have found
    you out.
The sparks of suspicion are melting your waters
And waters can't drown them, the fires are burning
And firemen can't calm them with falsely appeasing
And preachers can't pray with hopes for deceiving
Nor leaders deliver a lecture on losing
Nor teachers inform them the chosen are choosing
For now is the fire and fires won't answer
To logical reason and hopefully seeming
Hot flames must devour the kneeling and feeling
And torture the masters whose idiot pleading
Gets lost in the echoes of dancing and bleeding.
We have found you out, four faced farmers, we have found
    you out.
We have found you out, four faced America, we have found
    you out.

Liberation from the Affluent Society | *Herbert Marcuse*

I am very happy to see so many flowers here and that is why I want to remind you that flowers, by themselves, have no power whatsoever, other than the power of men and women who protect them and take care of them against aggression and destruction.

As a hopeless philosopher for whom philosophy has become inseparable from politics, I am afraid I have to give here today a rather philosophical speech, and I must ask your indulgence. We are dealing with the dialectics of liberation (actually a redundant phrase, because I believe that all dialectic is liberation) and not only liberation in an intellectual sense, but liberation involving the mind and the body, liberation involving entire human existence. Think of Plato: the liberation from the existence in the cave. Think of Hegel: liberation in the sense of progress and freedom on the historical scale. Think of Marx. Now in what sense is all dialectic liberation? It is liberation from the repressive, from a bad, a false system – be it an organic system, be it a social system, be it a mental or intellectual system: liberation by forces developing within such a system. That is a decisive point. And liberation by virtue of the contradiction generated by the system, precisely because it is a bad, a false system.

I am intentionally using here moral, philosophical terms, values: 'bad', 'false'. For without an objectively justifiable goal of a better, a free human existence, all liberation must remain meaningless – at best, progress in servitude. I believe that in Marx too socialism *ought* to be. This 'ought' belongs to the very essence of scientific socialism. It *ought* to be; it is, we may almost say, a biological, sociological and political necessity. It is a biological necessity in as much as a socialist society, according to Marx, would conform with the very *logos* of life, with the essential possibilities of a human existence, not only mentally, not only intellectually, but also organically.

Now as to today and our own situation. I think we are faced with a novel situation in history, because today we have to be liberated from a relatively well-functioning, rich, powerful society. I am speaking here about liberation from the affluent society, that is to say, the advanced industrial societies. The problem we are facing is the need for liberation not from a poor society, not from a disintegrating society, not even in most cases from a terroristic society, but from a society which develops to a great extent the material and even cultural needs of man – a society which, to use a slogan, delivers the goods to an ever larger part of the population. And that implies, we are facing liberation from a society where liberation is apparently without a mass basis. We know very well the social mechanisms of manipulation, indoctrination, repression which are responsible for this lack of a mass basis, for the integration of the majority of the oppositional forces into the established social system. But I must emphasize again that this is not merely an ideological integration; that it is not merely a social integration; that it takes place precisely on the strong and rich basis which enables the society to develop and satisfy material and cultural needs better than before.

But knowledge of the mechanisms of manipulation or repression, which go down into the very unconscious of man, is not the whole story. I believe that we (and I will use 'we' throughout my talk) have been too hesitant, that we have been too ashamed, understandably ashamed, to insist on the integral, radical features of a socialist society, its qualitative difference from all the established societies: the qualitative difference by virtue of which socialism is indeed the negation of the established systems, no matter how productive, no matter how powerful they are or they may appear. In other words – and this is one of the many points where I disagree with Paul Goodman – our fault was not that we have been too immodest, but that we have been too modest. We have, as it were, repressed a great deal of what we should have said and what we should have emphasized.

If today these integral features, these truly radical features which make a socialist society a definite negation of the existing societies, if this qualitative difference today appears as Utopian, as idealistic, as metaphysical, this is precisely the form in which these radical features must appear if they are really to be a definite negation of the established society: if socialism is indeed the rupture of history, the radical break, the leap into the realm of freedom – a total rupture.

Let us give one illustration of how this awareness, or half-awareness, of the need for such a total rupture was present in some of the great social struggles of our period. Walter Benjamin quotes reports that during the Paris Commune, in all corners of the city of Paris there were people shooting at the clocks on the towers of the churches, palaces and so on, thereby consciously or half-consciously expressing the need that somehow time has to be arrested; that at least the prevailing, the established time continuum has to be arrested, and that a new time has to begin – a very strong emphasis on the qualitative difference and on the totality of the rupture between the new society and the old.

In this sense, I should like to discuss here with you the repressed prerequisites of qualitative change. I say intentionally 'of qualitative change', not 'of revolution', because we know of too many revolutions through which the continuum of repression has been sustained, revolutions which have replaced one system of domination by another. We must become aware of the essentially new features which distinguish a free society as a definite negation of the established societies, and we must begin formulating these features, no matter how metaphysical, no matter how Utopian, I would even say no matter how ridiculous we may appear to the normal people in all camps, on the right as well as on the left.

What is the dialectic of liberation with which we here are concerned? It is the construction of a free society, a construction which depends in the first place on the prevalence of the vital need for abolishing the established systems of servitude; and secondly, and this is decisive, it depends on the vital commitment, the striving, conscious as well as sub- and un-conscious, for the qualitatively different values of a free human existence. Without the emergence of such new needs and satisfactions, the needs and satisfactions of free men, all change in the social institutions, no matter how great, would only replace one system of servitude by another system of servitude. Nor can the emergence – and I should like to emphasize this – nor can the emergence of such new needs and satisfactions be envisaged as a mere by-product, the mere result, of changed social institutions. We have seen this, it is a fact of experience. The development of the new institutions must already be carried out and carried through by men with the new needs. That, by the way, is the basic idea underlying Marx's own concept of the proletariat as the historical agent of revolution. He saw the industrial proletariat as the historical agent of revolution, not only because it was the basic class in the material process of production, not only because it was at that time the majority of the population, but also because this class was 'free' from the repressive and aggressive competitive needs of capitalist society and therefore, at least potentially, the carrier of essentially new needs, goals and satisfactions.

We can formulate this dialectic of liberation also in a more brutal way, as a vicious circle. The transition from voluntary servitude (as it exists to a great extent in the affluent society) to freedom presupposes the abolition of the institutions and mechanism of repression. And the abolition of the institutions and mechanisms of repression already presupposes liberation from servitude, prevalence of the need for liberation. As to needs, I think we have to distinguish between the need for changing intolerable conditions of existence, and the need for changing the society as a whole. The two are by no means identical, they are by no means in harmony. *If* the need is for changing intolerable conditions of existence, with at least a reasonable chance that this can be achieved within the established society, with the growth and progress of the established society, then this is merely quantitative change. Qualitative change is a change of the very system as a whole.

I would like to point out that the distinction between quantitative and qualitative change is not identical with the distinction between reform and revolution. Quantitative change can mean and can lead to revolution. Only the conjunction, I suggest, of these two is revolution in the essential sense of the leap from pre-history into the history of man. In other words, the problem with which we are faced is the point where quantity can turn into quality, where the quantitative change in the conditions and institutions can become a qualitative change affecting all human existence.

Today the two potential factors of revolution which I have just mentioned are disjointed. The first is most prevalent in the underdeveloped countries, where quantitative change – that is to say, the creation of human living conditions – is in itself qualitative change, but is not yet freedom. The second potential factor of revolution, the prerequisites of liberation, are potentially there in the advanced industrial countries, but are contained and perverted by the capitalist organization of society.

I think we are faced with a situation in which this

advanced capitalist soicety has reached a point where quantitative change can technically be turned into qualitative change, into authentic liberation. And it is precisely against this truly fatal possibility that the affluent society, advanced capitalism, is mobilized and organized on all fronts, at home as well as abroad.

Before I go on, let me give a brief definition of what I mean by an affluent society. A model, of course, is American society today, although even in the US it is more a tendency, not yet entirely translated into reality. In the first place, it is a capitalist society. It seems to be necessary to remind ourselves of this because there are some people, even on the left, who believe that American society is no longer a class society. I can assure you that it is a class society. It is a capitalist society with a high concentration of economic and political power; with an enlarged and enlarging sector of automation and coordination of production, distribution and communication; with private ownership in the means of production, which however depends increasingly on ever more active and wide intervention by the government. It is a society in which, as I mentioned, the material as well as cultural needs of the underlying population are satisfied on a scale larger than ever before – but they are satisfied in line with the requirements and interests of the apparatus and of the powers which control the apparatus. And it is a society growing on the condition of accelerating waste, planned obsolescence and destruction, while the substratum of the population continues to live in poverty and misery.

I believe that these factors are internally interrelated, that they constitute the syndrome of late capitalism: namely, the apparently inseparable unity – inseparable for the system – of productivity and destruction, of satisfaction of needs and repression, of liberty within a system of servitude – that is to say, the subjugation of man to the apparatus, and the inseparable unity of rational and irrational. We can say that the rationality of the society lies in its very insanity, and that the insanity of the society is rational to the degree to which it is efficient, to the degree to which it delivers the goods.

Now the question we must raise is: why do we need liberation from such a society if it is capable – perhaps in the distant future, but apparently capable – of conquering poverty to a greater degree than ever before, of reducing the toil of labour and the time of labour, and of raising the standard of living? If the price for all goods delivered, the price for this comfortable servitude, for all these achievements, is exacted from people far away from the metropolis and far away from its affluence? If the affluent society itself hardly notices what it is doing, how it is spreading terror and enslavement, how it is fighting liberation in all corners of the globe?

We know the traditional weakness of emotional, moral and humanitarian arguments in the face of such technological achievement, in the face of the irrational rationality of such a power. These arguments do not seem to carry any weight against the brute facts – we might say brutal facts – of the society and its productivity. And yet, it is only the insistence on the real possibilities of a free society, which is blocked by the affluent society – it is only this insistence in practice as well as in theory, in demonstration as well as in discussion, which still stands in the way of the complete degradation of man to an object, or rather subject/object, of total administration. It is only this insistence which still stands in the way of the progressive brutalization and moronization of man. For – and I should like to emphasize this – the capitalist Welfare State is a Warfare State. It must have an Enemy, with a capital E, a total Enemy; because the perpetuation of servitude, the perpetuation of the miserable struggle for existence in the very face of the new possibilities of freedom, activates and intensifies in this society a primary aggressiveness to a degree, I think, hitherto unknown in history. And this primary aggressiveness must be mobilized in socially useful ways, lest it explode the system itself. Therefore the need for an Enemy, who must be there, and who must be created if he does not exist. Fortunately, I dare say, the Enemy does exist. But his image and his power must, in this society, be inflated beyond all proportions in order to be able to mobilize this aggressiveness of the affluent society in socially useful ways.

The result is a mutilated, crippled and frustrated human existence: a human existence that is violently defending its own servitude.

We can sum up the fatal situation with which we are confronted. Radical social change is objectively necessary, in the dual sense that it is the only chance to save the possibilities of human freedom and, furthermore, in the sense that the technical and material resources for the realization of freedom are available. But while this objective need is demonstrably there, the subjective need for such a change does not prevail. It does not prevail precisely among those parts of the population that are traditionally considered the agents of historical change. The subjective need is repressed, again on a dual ground: firstly, by virtue of the actual satisfaction of needs, and secondly, by a massive scientific manipulation and administration of needs – that is, by a systematic social control not only of the consciousness, but also of the unconscious of man. This control has been made possible by the very achievements of the greatest liberating sciences of our time, in psychology, mainly psychoanalysis and psychiatry. That they could become and have become at the same time powerful instruments of suppression, one of the most effective engines of suppression, is again one of the terrible aspects of the dialectic of liberation.

This divergence between the objective and the subjective need changes completely, I suggest, the basis, the prospects and the strategy of liberation. This situation presupposes the emergence of new needs, qualitatively different and even opposed to the prevailing aggressive and repressive needs: the emergence of a new type of man, with a vital, biological drive for liberation, and with a consciousness capable of breaking through the material as well as ideological veil of the affluent society. In other words, liberation seems to be predicated upon the opening and the activation of a depth dimension of human existence, this side of and underneath the traditional material base: not an idealistic dimension, over and above the material base, but a dimension even more material than the material base, a dimension underneath the material base. I will illustrate presently what I mean.

The emphasis on this new dimension does not mean replacing politics by psychology, but rather the other way around. It means finally taking account of the fact that society has invaded even the deepest roots of individual existence, even the unconscious of man. *We* must get at the roots of society in the individuals themselves, the individuals who, because of social engineering, constantly reproduce the continuum of repression even through the great revolution.

This change is, I suggest, not an ideological change. It is dictated by the actual development of an industrial society, which has introduced factors which our theory could formerly correctly neglect. It is dictated by the actual development of industrial society, by the tremendous growth of its material and technical productivity, which has surpassed and rendered obsolete the traditional goals and preconditions of liberation.

Here we are faced with the question: is liberation from the affluent society identical with the transition from capitalism to socialism? The answer I suggest is: It is not identical, if socialism is defined merely as the planned development of the productive forces, and the rationalization of resources (although this remains a precondition for all liberation). It is identical with the transition from capitalism to socialism, if socialism is defined in its most Utopian terms: namely, among others, the abolition of labour, the termination of the struggle for existence – that is to say, life as an end in itself and no longer as a means to an end – and the liberation of human sensibility and sensitivity, not as a private factor, but as a force for transformation of human existence and of its environment. To give sensitivity and sensibility their own right is, I think, one of the basic goals of integral socialism. These are the qualitatively different features of a free society. They presuppose, as you may already have seen, a total trans-valuation of values, a new anthropology. They presuppose a type of man who rejects the performance principles governing the established societies; a type of man who has rid himself of the aggressiveness and brutality that are inherent in the organization of established society, and in their hypocritical, puritan morality; a type of man who is biologically incapable of fighting wars and creating suffering; a type of man who has a good conscience of joy and pleasure, and who works, collectively and individually, for a social and natural environment in which such an existence becomes possible.

The dialectic of liberation, as turned from quantity into quality, thus involves, I repeat, a break in the continuum of repression which reaches into the depth dimension of the organism itself. Or, we may say that today qualitative change, liberation, involves organic, instinctual, biological changes at the same time as political and social changes.

The new needs and satisfactions have a very material basis, as I have indicated. They are not thought out but are the logical derivation from the technical, material and intellectual possibilities of advanced, industrial society. They are inherent in, and the expression of, the productivity of advanced industrial society, which has long since made obsolete all kinds of inner-worldly asceticism, the entire work discipline on which Judaeo-Christian morality has been based.

Why is this society surpassing and negating this type of man, the traditional type of man, and the forms of his existence, as well as the morality to which it owes much of its origins and foundations? This new, unheard-of and not anticipated productivity allows the concept of a technology of liberation. Here I can only briefly indicate what I have in mind: such amazing and indeed apparently Utopian tendencies as the convergence of technique and art, the convergence of work and play, the convergence of the realm of necessity and the realm of freedom. How? No longer subjected to the dictates of capitalist profitability and of efficiency, no longer to the dictates of scarcity, which today are perpetuated by the capitalist organization of society; socially necessary labour, material production, would and could become (we see the tendency already) increasingly scientific. Technical experimentation, science and technology would and could become a play with the hitherto hidden – methodically hidden and blocked – potentialities of men and things, of society and nature.

This means one of the oldest dreams of all radical theory and practice. It means that the creative imagination, and not only the rationality of the performance principle, would become a productive force applied to the transformation of the social and natural universe. It would mean the emergence of a form of reality which is the work and the medium of the developing sensibility and sensitivity of man.

And now I throw in the terrible concept: it would mean an 'aesthetic' reality – society as a work of art. This is the most Utopian, the most radical possibility of liberation today.

What does this mean, in concrete terms? I said, we are not concerned here with private sensitivity and sensibility, but with sensitivity and sensibility, creative imagination and play, becoming forces of transformation. As such they would guide, for example, the total reconstruction of our cities and of the countryside; the restoration of nature after the elimination of the violence and destruction of capitalist industrialization; the creation of internal and external space for privacy, individual autonomy, tranquillity; the elimination of noise, of captive audiences, of enforced togetherness, of pollution, of ugliness. These are not – and I cannot emphasize this strongly enough – snobbish and romantic demands. Biologists today have emphasized that these are organic needs for the human organism, and that their arrest, their perversion and destruction by capitalist society, actually mutilates the human organism, not only in a figurative way but in a very real and literal sense.

I believe that it is only in such a universe that man can be truly free, and truly human relationships between free beings can be established. I believe that the idea of such a universe guided also Marx's concept of socialism, and that these aesthetic needs and goals must from the beginning be present in the reconstruction of society, and not only at the end or in the far future. Otherwise, the needs and satisfactions which reproduce a repressive society would be carried over into the new society. Repressive men would carry over their repression into the new society.

Now, at this farthest point, the question is: how can we possibly envisage the emergence of such qualitatively different needs and goals as organic, biological needs and goals and not as superimposed values? How can we envisage the emergence of these needs and satisfactions within and against the established society – that is to say, prior to liberation? That was the dialectic with which I started, that in a very definite sense we have to be free from in order to create a free society.

Needless to say, the dissolution of the existing system is

the precondition for such qualitative change. And the more efficiently the repressive apparatus of the affluent societies operates, the less likely is a gradual transition from servitude to freedom. The fact that today we cannot identify any specific class or any specific group as a revolutionary force, this fact is no excuse for not using any and every possibility and method to arrest the engines of repression in the individual. The diffusion of potential opposition among the entire underlying population corresponds precisely to the total character of our advanced capitalist society. The internal contradictions of the system are as grave as ever before and likely to be aggravated by the violent expansion of capitalist imperialism. Not only the most general contradictions between the tremendous social wealth on the one hand, and the destructive, aggressive and wasteful use of this wealth on the other; but far more concrete contradictions such as the necessity for the system to automate, the continued reduction of the human base in physical labour-power in the material reproduction of society and thereby the tendency towards the draining of the sources of surplus profit. Finally, there is the threat of technological unemployment which even the most affluent society may no longer be capable of compensating by the creation of ever more parasitic and unproductive labour: all these contradictions exist. In reaction to them suppression, manipulation and integration are likely to increase.

But fulfilment is there, the ground can and must be prepared. The mutilated consciousness and the mutilated instincts must be broken. The sensitivity and the awareness of the new transcending, antagonistic values – they are there. And they are there, they are here, precisely among the still non-integrated social groups and among those who, by virtue of their privileged position, can pierce the ideological and material veil of mass communication and indoctrination – namely, the intelligentsia.

We all know the fatal prejudice, practically from the beginning, in the Labour Movement against the intelligentsia as catalyst of historical change. It is time to ask whether this prejudice against the intellectuals, and the inferiority complex of the intellectuals resulting from it, was not an essential factor in the development of the capitalist as well as the socialist societies: in the development and weakening of the opposition. The intellectuals usually went out to organize the others, to organize in the communities. They certainly did not use the potentiality they had to organize themselves, to organize among themselves not only on a regional, not only on a national, but on an international level. That is, in my view, today one of the most urgent tasks. Can we say that the intelligentsia is the agent of historical change? Can we say that the intelligentsia today is a revolutionary class? The answer I would give is: No, we cannot say that. But we can say, and I think we must say, that the intelligentsia has a decisive preparatory function, not more; and I suggest that this is plenty. By itself it is not and cannot be a revolutionary class, but it can become the catalyst, and it has a preparatory function – certainly not for the first time, that is in fact the way all revolution starts – but more, perhaps, today than ever before. Because – and for this too we have a very material and very concrete basis – it is from this group that the holders of decisive positions in the productive process will be recruited, in the future even more than hitherto. I refer to what we may call the increasingly scientific character of the material process of production, by virtue of which the role of the intelligentsia changes. It is the group from which the decisive holders of decisive positions will be recruited: scientists, researchers, technicians, engineers, even psychologists – because psychology will continue to be a socially necessary instrument, either of servitude or of liberation.

This class, this intelligentsia has been called the new

working class. I believe this term is at best premature. They are – and this we should not forget – today the pet beneficiaries of the established system. But they are also at the very source of the glaring contradictions between the liberating capacity of science and its repressive and enslaving use. To activate the repressed and manipulated contradiction, to make it operate as a catalyst of change, that is one of the main tasks of the opposition today. It remains and must remain a political task.

Education is our job, but education in a new sense. Being theory as well as practice, political practice, education today is more than discussion, more than teaching and learning and writing. Unless and until it goes beyond the classroom, until and unless it goes beyond the college, the school, the university, it will remain powerless. Education today must involve the mind *and* the body, reason *and* imagination, the intellectual *and* the instinctual needs, because our entire existence has become the subject/object of politics, of social engineering. I emphasize, it is not a question of making the schools and universities, of making the educational system political. The educational system is political already. I need only remind you of the incredible degree to which (I am speaking of the US) universities are involved in huge research grants (the nature of which you know in many cases) by the government and the various quasi-governmental agencies.

The educational system *is* political, so it is not we who want to politicize the educational system. What we want is a counter-policy against the established policy. And in this sense we must meet this society on its own ground of total mobilization. We must confront indoctrination in servitude with indoctrination in freedom. We must each of us generate in ourselves, and try to generate in others, the instinctual need for a life without fear, without brutality, and without stupidity. And we must see that we can generate the instinctual and intellectual revulsion against the values of an affluence which spreads aggressiveness and suppression throughout the world.

Before I conclude I would like to say my bit about the Hippies. It seems to me a serious phenomenon. If we are talking of the emergence of an instinctual revulsion against the values of the affluent society, I think here is a place where we should look for it. It seems to me that the Hippies, like any non-conformist movement on the left, are split. That there are two parts, or parties, or tendencies. Much of it is mere masquerade and clownery on the private level, and therefore indeed, as Gerassi suggested, completely harmless, very nice and charming in many cases, but that is all there is to it. But that is not the whole story. There is in the Hippies, and especially in such tendencies in the Hippies as the Diggers and the Provos, an inherent political element – perhaps even more so in the US than here. It is the appearance indeed of new instinctual needs and values. This experience is there. There is a new sensibility against efficient and insane reasonableness. There is the refusal to play the rules of a rigid game, a game which one knows is rigid from the beginning, and the revolt against the compulsive cleanliness of puritan morality and the aggression bred by this puritan morality as we see it today in Vietnam among other things.

At least this part of the Hippies, in which sexual, moral and political rebellion are somehow united, is indeed a non-aggressive form of life: a demonstration of an aggressive non-aggressiveness which achieves, at least potentially, the demonstration of qualitatively different values, a transvaluation of values.

All education today is therapy: therapy in the sense of liberating man by all available means from a society in which, sooner or later, he is going to be transformed into a brute, even if he doesn't notice it any more. Education in this sense is therapy, and all therapy today is political theory and practice. What kind of political practice? That depends entirely on the situation. It is hardly imaginable that we should discuss this here in detail. I will only remind you of the various possibilities of demonstrations, of finding out flexible modes of demonstration which can cope with the use of institutionalized violence, of boycott, many other things – anything goes which is such that it indeed has a reasonable chance of strengthening the forces of the opposition.

We can prepare for it as educators, as students. Again I say, our role is limited. We are no mass movement. I do not believe that in the near future we will see such a mass movement.

I want to add one word about the so-called Third World. I have not spoken of the Third World because my topic was strictly liberation from the affluent society. I agree entirely with Paul Sweezy, that without putting the affluent society in the framework of the Third World it is not understandable. I also believe that here and now our emphasis must be on the advanced industrial societies – not forgetting to do whatever we can and in whatever way we can to support, theoretically and practically, the struggle for liberation in the neo-colonial countries which, if again they are not the final force of liberation, at least contribute their share – and it is a considerable share – to the potential weakening and disintegration of the imperialist world system.

Our role as intellectuals is a limited role. On no account should we succumb to any illusions. But even worse than this is to succumb to the wide-spread defeatism which we witness. The preparatory role today is an indispensable role. I believe I am not being too optimistic – I have not in general the reputation of being too optimistic – when I say that we can already see the signs, not only that *They* are getting frightened and worried but that there are far more concrete, far more tangible manifestations of the essential weakness of the system. Therefore, let us continue with whatever we can – no illusions, but even more, no defeatism.

Beyond Words | *David Cooper*

At this Congress during the last two weeks we have been oscillating between various antitheses. The Congress was supposed to be about dialectics, but the whole point about dialectics is that one has to be the dialectics that one is about, and then to know that this is what it is all about anyhow.

So let me point to various dialectics that have been going on here in the Roundhouse.

For instance, there has been the oscillation between the theoretical, contemplative pole (with its hidden dimension of action) represented by Gregory Bateson, and then the political activistic pole (which has a less evident dimension of theory) represented by, say, Stokely Carmichael. An index of the success we have achieved in the living out of this dialectic might be little more than the simple fact that people engaged in dealing with such contrasted aspects of reality have found it possible, not only to last out their full agreed term at the Congress, but also to live under the same roof for most of their time here. But I think that more than that has been accomplished. I think that a subtle extension of awareness has been happening in people that will not issue immediately in alterations of political or scientific posture, but which will, I think, become retrospectively evident in the history of these next decades or so.

Then let us look at another dialectic. We have moved between the pole of detailed, concrete study of the lives of individuals, families and networks, and the pole represented by the study of the anonymous, large-scale, social-political event.

There are so many false solutions to this problem of

mediation. Let me mention just two that have been suggested to me recently – in fact at this Congress. One was that anti-psychiatrists should elect to see only those people who could turn them on politically so that the anti-psychiatrists could then potentiate the political activism of these people. The other was that anti-psychiatrists should cut across the mythical, socially invented neurosis of their patients and deflect them into the emerging new revolutionary groups – so that schizophrenia could be used against those social manipulators who had in fact invented it as a disease. But these are false solutions. Before we propose answers we have to be quite sure that we have the question because, once again, the answer is in the question when the question is fully formed in our minds and bodies. That is dialectic.

Another dialectic that has been clearly demonstrated here is the dialectic that has as one pole the horizontal study of structures that assumes one can cut across social time and then say things about the hypothetical moment one has apparently isolated. The other proposed pole, the vertical one, is a sort of historical reductionism that is exemplified by the worst sort of psycho-analysis and by academic history ('white history' as Stokely Carmichael has called it) – history that merely chronicles events while pretending to do more than this – but all it does is to re-affirm ruling-class values in a respectable enough way. Now, we have seen this dialectic make nonsense of the fictional antagonisms of both structuralism and naïve historicism.

What other dialectics have been going on here? Let me suggest one that may be more immediately real to many people here – people who have, I hope, suffered rather than enjoyed the daily ritual of lectures and who have then sweated through the seminars, films, special presentations, panels, workshops and so on.

During this fortnight we have, at least some of us, moved

from the position of compulsive speaking – you know, the spectacle every morning after the main lecture of two queues of people with their hands outstretched for the microphone on either side – I think we've moved on a bit from that.

The position that we have moved on to is one in which silence, at first vociferously demanded, has now, for a number of people here, become a matter of constant option. We may now opt, on the basis of our acquired capacities, for the jewel of silence, for the possibility of a non-refusing personal aloneness. This seems to me to be the precondition of reasonable discourse.

By reasonable discourse I mean a way of talking not to but with each other, a manner of speech that simply makes the constant promise of transforming some segment of the world that we commonly, or communally, between us, experience.

Related to this there is one image from this Congress out of many impressive images that will always remain preeminent in my mind. Stokely Carmichael was being repetitively criticized for his frank and total abandonment of white liberal 'support' and the 'support' of the so-called moderate black leadership. Stokely stood there, shaking his finger at the questioners, asking over and over again : 'What have you *done*? ... What *have* you done? ... What have *you* done?'

Of course he was accused of not answering the questions, but we should now begin to realize that the answer was *his* question. Our task, as this has been exhaustively spelt out, is not to try to help him but to effect the erosion of what he calls white power. There is nothing racistic about that *if one realizes that there is in the world a contingent but not necessary identity of white power and imperialism.* This, I think, is absolutely crucial to the difficulties that many people seem to have with Stokely Carmichael's stance. It is on the basis of a misunderstanding of this pivotal distinction that some people have concluded that the ideology of Carmichael's position is a sort of counter-racism. The essence of Stokely Carmichael's position is, I think, fairly clear to us now. It is the passionate recognition, reinforced by detailed analysis of the situation, that the condition of black people in the USA is in a relation of direct continuity with the condition of people in the Third World struggling towards their liberation.

This is quite central to the strategy of their struggle for justice, but it is also very illuminating for us in the first world. Illuminating for us when we come to consider what we may do. I hope that the emissaries of the Home Secretary present here today will duly carry this message back to Roy Jenkins. If they do just this they will have well earned the salaries that we are paying them for their work here today!

We are not oppressed by this force – white power-imperialism – in the same way that the Third World (including black people in the US) is, *but we are oppressed by it*. What we have to do is to recognize how we are oppressed, to feel the violence of this oppression as a vitalizing despair – as a despair that refuses to subside into the desperation that proposes cutting across this reality by putting psychedelic drugs in the water supply and blowing up power stations in the US. There are no short cuts. What we have to do beyond the monumental task of perceiving the Third World as it is, in itself, is perceive the more obscure reality of the presence of the Third World *in us*.

When we become conscious of our oppression we have to invent the strategy and tactics of our guerrilla warfare. We deracinated white intellectuals, we who are bourgeois and colonizing in essence even though some of us wear the spurious label of 'working-class origin' – we must realize that we cannot pretend to engage in clandestine operations aimed at subverting the system because we have not been bred in that sort of struggle. Certainly we have to keep some secrets, but on the whole our scene is illuminated by all the forms of artificial lighting that issue from our culture.

What we have to do quite simply is to deploy all our personal resources in attacking the institutionalization of experience and action in *this* society. We have one advantage over our rulers – we have a consciousness, although only marginal at times, of what is going on in the world; we see through their mystifications – the mystifications that mystify the mystifiers but need no longer mystify us. By a transactional network of expertise we can transform each institution – family, school, university, mental hospital, factory – each art form, into a revolutionary centre for a transforming consciousness. We recognize that the socialist countries in Eastern Europe are in much the same case as us. We must recognize that revolution in the sense of the socialist transformation of economic life and social forms does not automatically entail changes in actual persons; the same alienations carry over, the same murderous bureaucracy continues – often in a caricatured form, as in Stalinism. External revolution does not entail inner revolution. We can take over the state apparatus and effect socialist changes and yet feel no better for having done this – no reality of liberation, beyond the transient liberating feeling of the struggle to do this. It seems to me that it is partly a self-concealed recognition of this truth that has stopped some powerful European working-class movements from taking power – this together with the confusing diffusion from them of oppression into the Third World; the praxis that has pushed the European working class out of their true class position.

If we persist with the theme of transformation of our institutions into revolutionary centres of consciousness, we have to be clear about why more has not been achieved by what we have already done in this way. The most immediate answer is that we have become victims of a very old colonizing technique – the technique of divide and rule. Innovators in the fields of education, psychiatry, all the arts and sciences, have been atomized, split off from other people doing much the same thing in some other area. In this way we lay ourselves open to the strategy of engulfment into the monolithic bourgeois bureaucratic system, with the consequence that we get ourselves invalidated and suppressed if we carry innovation 'too far'.

To move out of this position we have to realize certain elementary truths about how we unconsciously perpetuate this structure that castrates us. We seem to have some curious paranoid passion to convert certain unlikely people into being the regulators of ourselves, so that we can hate and despise them as the bureaucrats who frustrate our genius. So we have to recognize that their power, the power of governments in the first world and, to a significant extent, in the European socialist world – their power is nothing less than our power. Our power, that we have perversely put into them, because we choose impotence.

If we re-interiorize our exteriorized power by uniting in our cultural revolution, we shall soon see what is left of them. We shall see men who have dehumanized themselves and would further dehumanize us. We shall see men who are terrorized by the vision of human autonomy and spontaneity.

So we see governments that we have to destructure and then lead in the direction of our liberation and incidentally theirs. This is what we have to do about the Third World – we have to liberate not them but us. No doubt we shall suffer in doing this, but I think we shall have the compensation of the surprising realization that we can actually enjoy doing it.

I would now like to propose to you a schema that I find

useful in considering questions of human identity – questions that must precede any planning for action.

Each of us is composed of a series of dualities that run through every level and form of our existence – from social persona, through the biological to the metaphysical and the mystical. These dualities include: subject–object; white–black; oppressor–oppressed one; colonizer–colonized; torturer–tortured; murderer–murdered one; psychiatrist–patient; teacher–taught; keeper–kept; the cannibal–the one who is eaten up; the fucker–the fucked; the shitter–the shitted-upon.

Now the ideal possibility here is that we contain all these oppositions and learn to bear both the pain and the joy of this act of self-containment. But, because of the historical situation, for which we are each of us totally responsible, we have each of us split any number of these dualities within us and have externalized these split-off aspects of ourselves into others. This supreme irrationality, which consists in blinding ourselves to the divisions that we achieve in ourselves so that we can extrude some painful bit of ourselves into others, this is the existential basis of colonialism, for instance, or institutionalized racism, or conventional psychiatry, or ordinary university education.

I am not getting into some sort of psychologism here, but I do think we have to eliminate the crude mechanistic idea of economic infra-structure and psychological and social supra-structure. There is in fact a constantly changing dialectical relationship between all these elements. Do we have to submit to the compulsion to hierarchize a structure that can then only become sclerosed, fossilized, dead?

What happens then is that we have a game situation in which there is a pay-off both for the one who seems to be at the better end of the thing and for the one who is at the less fortunate end. The pay-off is that one has one's identity defined by the other and then one has the security of knowing precisely who, what and where one is – or so one thinks. The value of this sort of ludic and ludicrous self-certainty often outstrips any question of advantage or disadvantage in terms of material things. This is proven repeatedly in history – for instance the game of white master and black slave which until now has been played out with only occasional and exceptional protests in the USA. If you are a black slave, at least you know where you stand. But then, if you take what at first seems to be an immense risk, you begin to question this whole game structure. You begin to ask who defines you by forming and controlling the rules of the game. This brings us back to a central point made by Stokely Carmichael recently – a point that must never get lost in the rhetoric of activism – I mean the question: who defines whom?

It seems to me that now, in this year, this question is posed more clearly than ever before. The question was posed some years ago in terms of the Algerian war of liberation, and J.-P. Sartre was one of the main protagonists of this type of analysis. It has been more and more explicitly posed in statements about the Vietnam war of liberation. The Vietnamese are the receptacles for all the split-off bad aspects of the US. They are the vicious, hypersexual, aggressive, subverting, offensive aspect that the White House and the Pentagon refuse to recognize in themselves. If you want to know what psychosis is, it is precisely this sort of mutilation of reality. Psychiatry seems however to know nothing of it.

If we are to define our predicament in Europe and North America, I think that this must be in terms of the loss of vision entailed by the increasing differentiation of experience and the delimitation and compartmentalization of forms of action entailed by this differentiation of experience.

This is very much the problem that we pose ourselves when we label anyone schizophrenic. Schizophrenia is a half-compelled, half-chosen retreat from the precariously and artificially stabilized level of highly differentiated experience that passes as sane in our culture at this time. Schizophrenia is simply the project – usually an abortive one thanks to social interference – to rediscover a pristine wholeness that really lies outside one's history but which is pointed to by one's history. This wholeness undercuts the differentiation of experience. It undercuts all the false divisions within and between arts and sciences, and the whole process of bringing people up – education.

So we have to overcome the false disciplines and find the true discipline. Schizophrenia is an abortive and always aborted attempt to achieve some degree of this sort of sanity. For real craziness we have to search the palaces of our rulers. Then we very soon find it.

A year or two ago I witnessed a happening in which an obsessionally arranged pile of books was burnt – it was, I think, a German philosophical dictionary in twenty volumes. This was a perfectly reasonable protest against institutionalized pseudo-scholarship, but it is not the most relevant sort of happening that we can put on. It might be more relevant to centre on the principle vehicles of mystification – mass-communication media. Perhaps we could, for instance, publicly tear up our daily newspapers (we can certainly read them first if we know how to read them!) and make bonfires of television sets and radios (with police permission, of course). And then we can tear up our ballot-papers in the next elections. At this historical juncture it seems important to let other people know that we don't pretend to elect those manipulators who pretend they are elected by some sort of unconditioned free choice.

In the meantime let us get on with consolidating the forms of collaboration that have become visible as possibilities here in the Roundhouse. Groups all over the world are doing something much the same as some of us are doing here in London, and we want to get this transnational network established so that people can move around from one centre to another, and then transform other centres into this potential for revolutionary consciousness.

I was very impressed with a story that Herbert Marcuse told us. During the Paris Commune, before they started shooting at people, the Communards shot at the clocks, at all the clocks in Paris, and they broke them. And they did this because they were putting an end to the time of the Others, the time of their rulers, and they were going to invent their own time.

As I look around me now I see a vista beyond your sea of faces, going way out there I see a vista of broken clocks. And now I think, it is our time!

Notes on Contributors

David Cooper

David Cooper was born in Cape Town, South Africa, in 1931. He graduated from the University of Cape Town in 1955 and then came to London, where he held a series of hospital posts. In the last of these he directed the experimental unit for young schizophrenics called Villa 21. His principal concern has been to develop existential psychiatry in Britain and to elaborate principles to overcome the methodological difficulties and compartmentalization of the human sciences. He is a founder member of the Philadelphia Association, London, and Director of the Institute of Phenomenological Studies. Among his works are *Reason and Violence* (with R. D. Laing) and *Psychiatry and Anti-Psychiatry*.

R. D. Laing

Ronald Laing was born in Glasgow in 1927. Psychiatrist (British Army, Glasgow Royal Mental Hospital, Dept of Psychological Medicine, Glasgow University, Tavistock Clinic, London) and psychoanalyst. He summarizes his work as research into the phenomenology of psychotic experience and psychedelics, and studies of the patterns of interaction in families. He is a founder member and Chairman of the Philadelphia Association, London, which has established three communities in London where people diagnosed as schizophrenic and others live in households which are entirely non-institutional settings. Among his books are *The Divided Self* (Pelican, 1965); *Sanity, Madness and the Family – Vol. I Families of Schizophrenics* (with A. Esterson) and *The Politics of Experience* (Penguin, 1967).

Gregory Bateson

Gregory Bateson has done anthropological field work in New Britain, New Guinea and Bali. Interest in patterning and family structure in other cultures led him to study the formal characteristics of various forms of mental illness. From 1950 to 1963 he worked with the Veterans Administration Hospital, Palo Alto, California, on the meaningful behaviour of schizophrenics and on the organizational patterns of families containing schizophrenics. Currently Bateson has shifted his focus of attention from the natural history of people to that of dolphins. He is with the Oceanic Institute, Oahu, Hawaii. His writings include *Balinese Character: A Photographic Analysis* (with Margaret Mead); *Communication: The Social Matrix of Psychiatry*; *Perceval's Narrative: A Patient's Account of his Psychosis, 1830-32.*

Jules Henry

Jules Henry states: 'I am interested in the relationship between sanity and insanity on the one hand, and the general condition of man on the other. In studying this relationship I have relied largely on the following approaches: historical materialism; the Hegelian dialectic; existentialism as represented by Kierkegaard, primarily, and then by Heidegger; phenomenology, deriving largely from Husserl; psychoanalysis; perception theory.' Currently he is professor of anthropology and sociology at the University of St Louis, USA. 'I think the only publication of mine relevant to the Congress is, perhaps, *Culture Against Man.*'

John Gerassi

John Gerassi was born in the United States. He has advanced degrees in philosophy and has been the Latin American editor of *Time* and *Newsweek*. He has taught philosophy and political science at Berkeley, the New School for Social Research, and Windham College. He has taught at the Free University of New York and is currently Professor of Political Science at San Francisco State College.

He is the author of a definitive study of American imperialism in Latin America entitled *The Great Fear in Latin America*.

Paul Sweezy

Paul Sweezy was born in New York, 1910. After graduating from Harvard he did one year of graduate study at the London School of Economics, and then returned to Harvard as Instructor, and later as Assistant Professor of Economics. During the Second World War he served in the Office of Strategic Services, and since then has been Visiting Professor of Economics at Cornell University, Stanford University and the New School for Social Research. He is currently Editor of *Monthly Review*. He has written many books including, with Paul A. Baran: *Monopoly Capital: An Essay on the American Economic and Social Order* (Pelican, 1968).

Paul Goodman

Paul Goodman was born in New York, 1911. He graduated from the City College of New York and took his Ph.D. in Humanities at the University of Chicago. He is a Fellow of the Institute for Gestalt Therapy and the Institute of Policy Studies, Washington, DC. He has taught at the University of Chicago and Wisconsin, and at Sarah Lawrence College and Black Mountain College. He is Editor of *Liberation*, and describes his position as anarchist-decentralist. His major works include: *Communitas* (with Percival Goodman), *Growing Up Absurd*, and *Community of Scholars*.

Lucien Goldmann

Professor Goldmann was born in 1913 in Bucharest. He studied law in Bucharest, literature in Vienna and Zurich, and in Paris, where he graduated as Docteur des Lettres. After working at the Centre National de la Recherche Scientifique, he went to the École Pratique dese Hautes Études, of which he is now Directeur d'Études. He is a leading member of the Neo-Structuralists school of thought in France. Among his many

studies is *Le Dieu Caché,* published in English under the title
The Hidden God.

Stokely Carmichael

(Student Non-Violent Coordinating Committee) SNCC Chairman Stokely Carmichael, 25, was raised in the slums of
Trinidad, the West Indies, New York City and Washington,
DC, where he attended Howard University. Toughened by
his ghetto life, Carmichael was a militant leader of Howard
University Student Government and gave direction and leadership to the student activist group in Washington called the
Nonviolent Action Group. Arrested over twelve times while
participating in Movement activities, Carmichael has seen
action in Jackson, Mississippi; New Orleans, Louisiana; Ten-
nessee; Maryland; Virginia; New York and Alabama. He has
worked with SNCC since its conception. When asked why
he joined the Movement and wanted to work with SNCC,
Carmichael said, 'I believe that while most other organizations
are working for reform, SNCC is trying to lay the foundation
for a revolution. I do not feel that a reform movement will
solve the socio-economic problems facing us ...' His book,
Black Power (with Charles Hamilton), appeared in 1967.

Herbert Marcuse

Herbert Marcuse was born in 1898 in Berlin. He graduated
from the University of Freiburg, emigrated from Germany in
1933 and after a brief spell at the Institut de Recherches Sociales
in Geneva went to the USA to the Institute of Social Research
at Columbia University. During the Second World War he
served at the Office of Strategic Services, Washington, and
lectured at the American University there. Thereafter he held
posts at Columbia University, Harvard and Yale, and from
1954 to 1965 was Professor of Politics and Philosophy at Bran-
deis University. During this period he also held posts at the
École Pratique des Hautes Études, Paris. He is now Professor
of Philosophy at the University of California. His principal

works include: *Reason and Revolution: Hegel and the Rise of Social Theory*; *Eros and Civilisation: A Philosophical Inquiry into Freud*; *One-Dimensional Man: Studies in Advanced Industrial Society*.

Dialectics of Liberation Records

The presentations in this book and other major discussions at the Congress are available as *12″ longplay phonograph records* as follows:

Each record £1. 5. 11   USA & Canada $2.99
Entire Set £30. 10. 0   USA & Canada $64.99

Order from: The Institute of Phenomenological Studies, 1 Sherwood Street, London W.1.